THE EYES OF TEXAS TRAVEL GUIDE

Dallas/East Texas Edition

THE EYES OF TEXAS
TRAVEL GUIDE
Dallas/East Texas Edition

By Ray Miller

with a comprehensive map of the Dallas/East Texas area

© Cordovan Corporation, Publishers
Houston 1978

Compiled and edited by the news department of KPRC-TV, Houston

EYES OF TEXAS TRAVEL GUIDE
Dallas and East Texas Edition
First Printing October 1978

Library of Congress Catalog Number: 78-67186
ISBN: 0-89123-056-4
Cover design by Russell Jumonville
Maps by Anita Schmoekel

Contents

Foreword

Ray Miller, in his "Eyes of Texas" television series, has made Texas history interesting to viewers of all ages. With his accompanying narrations, he has brought our heritage alive. In recording the past he has painted visions for the future.

The "Eyes of Texas" has depicted on film more historic places and interesting people than any other program in the history of our State. It has included the story of Texas heroes and builders, natural resources and scenery, sites of early settlements, homes, missions and churches, schools, courthouses, battlefields, cemeteries, oil booms, industries, agriculture, and just about everything representative of our glorious past and our promising future.

It was inevitable that Ray Miller's television series would lead to the publication of "Eyes of Texas Travel Guides." Thousands of listeners and viewers of the narrated film wanted to see some of it preserved on the printed page, together with directions for finding and seeing the places and subjects.

The first *Eyes of Texas Travel Guide,* Gulf Coast Edition, is now in its sixth printing. It covers 30 counties, including seven in Southeast Texas. This East Texas Edition covers the remainder of East Texas. I recommend it to all who want to know and to see this historic and important area of Texas, and I congratulate Ray Miller and his staff for another job well done.

Price Daniel, Sr.
Former Governor of Texas

Introduction

There are differing views about what part of Texas is properly called East Texas.

For the purposes of this book, East Texas is the territory along and east of Interstate Highway 45 and U.S. 75, to the Red River on the north to the Louisiana state line on the east and bounded on the south by the northern boundaries of the counties included in the original "Eyes of Texas Travel Guide, Gulf Coast Edition." We have included Dallas but not Fort Worth or Houston.

The section of the state we have defined as East Texas includes some of the most modern architecture in the world and some of the oldest in Texas. It includes four busy interstate highways and some of the most tranquil backroads you can find anywhere. It includes some of the state's most historic settlements, an Indian Reservation, four national forests and dozens of lakes. It is the best of Texas in the eyes of many Texans.

DEDICATION

We are indebted to the Texas Department of Highways and Public Transportation, the Department of Parks and Wildlife, the Texas Historical Commission, The Texas Historical Assn., The HANDBOOK OF TEXAS, The Texas State Library, the Historical Societies of the various counties, the Houston Public Library, and the numerous individuals for helping us gather the information for our television program and for this book. We dedicate this volume to all of them.

Ray Miller and the staff of the "Eyes of Texas".
Houston, Texas
August 1978

Durant
Lake Texhoma
Red River
Denison
Sherman
Whitesboro
Lake Kiowa
Southmayd
Collinsville
Tioga
Pilot Point
Denton
Garza-Little Elm Res.
Lewisville
Grapevine Lake
Euless
Irving
Arlington
Grand Prairie
Duncanville
Cedar Hill
Venus
Midlothian
Farmers Branch
Carrollton
DALLAS
Dallas
Richardson
Garland
Mesquite
Balch Springs
Seagoville
Kleberg
Hutchins
Lancaster
Ferris
Red Oak
Palmer
ELLIS
Waxahachie
Forreston
Italy
Avalon
Bardwell
Bardwell Lake
Ennis
Alma
Rice
GRAYSON
Gunter
Van Alstyne
Tom Bean
Howe
Whitewright
Bells
Savoy
Ector
Randolph
Trenton
Leonard
Bailey
FANNIN
Bonham
Lake Bonham
Dodd City
Windom
Honey Grove
Petty
Ladonia
Celina
COLLIN
McKinney
Anna
Melissa
Blue Ridge
Celeste
Wolfe City
Fairlie
Commerce
Kingston
Neylandville
Princeton
Farmersville
Greenville
Lavon Lake
Allen
Plano
Wylie
Lavon
Copeville
Caddo Mills
HUNT
Campbell
Cash
Royse City
Rockwall
ROCKWALL
Quinlan
Lake Ray Hubbard
Forney
Terrell
Elmo
Kaufman
Crandall
KAUFMAN
Scurry
Rosser
Kemp
Tolosa
Seven Points
Cedar Creek Reservoir
Tool
Kerens
Powell
Trinidad
Malakoff
Athens
Eustace
Mabank
Phalba
Murchison
Brownsboro
Chandler
Lake Athens
Coffee City
Larue
Lake Palestine
Bullard
Whitehouse
Mount Selman
Troup
Lake Tyler
Tyler
SMITH
Overton
Arp
Turnertown
Price
New London
Kilgore
Lakeport
Lake Cherokee
RUSK
Chapman
Martin Creek Lake
Henderson
Clayton
Beckville
Tatum
Carthage
PANOLA
De Berry
Panola
Joaquin
Logansport
Murval Reservoir
Paris
Lake Crook
Pat Mayse Lake
Arthur City
Powderly
Toco
Reno
Blossom
Sun Valley
Pattonville
Deport
LAMAR
Detroit
RED RIVER
Clarksville
Negley
Avery
Bogata
Johntown
Talco
DELTA
Cooper
HOPKINS
Ridgeway
Sulphur Springs
Brashear
Como
Pickton
Weaver
Saltillo
Hagansport
FRANKLIN
Mount Vernon
Winfield
Lake Cypress Springs
Lake Monticello
TITUS
Mount Pleasant
Cookville
Omaha
MORRIS
Naples
Daingerfield
Hughes Spring
Pittsburg
Leesburg
Newsome
CAMP
Winnsboro
WOOD
Yantis
Lone Oak Point
Lake Tawakoni
Emory
RAINS
Alba
Lake Quitman
Lake Winnsboro
Quitman
Sabine River
Grand Saline
Lake Holbrook
Mineola
Edgewood
Fruitvale
Wills Point
Myrtle Springs
Canton
VAN ZANDT
Van
Garden Valley
Lindale
Ben Wheeler
Mount Sylvan
Lake Hawkins
Crow
Hawkins
Big Sandy
Winona
Gladewater
Lake Gladewater
West Mountain
Glenwood
Pritchett
Gilmer
UPSHUR
Bettie
Ore City
Diana
GREGG
Longview
Harleton
Hallsville
Marshall
HARRISON
Woodlawn
Karnack
Caddo Lake
Jonesville
Waskom
Mooringsport
Jefferson
Lake O' the Pines
Lone Star
Ellison Creek Res.
Cason
Avinger
CASS
MARION
Smithland
Linden
Bivins
Atlanta
Queen City
Bloomburg
Douglassville
Lake Patman
Maud
Bassett
Simms
Redwater
BOWIE
DeKalb
Malta
New Boston
Boston
Old Boston
Hooks
Leary
Nash
Wake Village
Texarkana
Ashdown
Idabel
Rodessa
McLeod
Vivian

LEGEND
20 Interstate Highway
190 U.S. Highway
110 19 State Highway
Scale of Miles
0 5 10 20 30 40 50
N
CHEROKEE
ANDERSON
FREESTONE
LEON
HOUSTON
NACOGDOCHES
SAN AUGUSTINE
SABINE
ANGELINA
TRINITY
TYLER
POLK
WALKER
MADISON
SAN JACINTO
MONTGOMERY
Bryan
College Station
Navasota
Hempstead
Huntsville
Conroe
Cleveland
Livingston
Woodville
Jasper
Lufkin
Nacogdoches
Crockett
Palestine
Centerville
Madisonville
Buffalo
Fairfield
Mexia
Groesbeck
Teague
Wortham
Coolidge
Hubbard
Center
Shelbyville
San Augustine
Hemphill
Pineland
Brookeland
Huntington
Diboll
Corrigan
Groveton
Trinity
Rusk
Alto
Elkhart
Grapeland
Kennard
Lovelady
Leona
Normangee
North Zulch
Kurten
Benchley
Dew
Jewett
Marquez
Kossee
Ridge
Easterly
Montalba
Neches
Maydelle
Cushing
Garrison
Melrose
Martinsville
Douglass
Sacul
Trawick
Slocum
Tucker
Long Lake
Oakwood
Donnie
Personville
Dawson
Malone
Streetman
Tehuacana
Lake Mexia
Lake Fairfield
Trinity River
Navasota River
Houston County Lake
Nacogdoches Lake
Toledo Bend Reservoir
Sam Rayburn Reservoir
Steinhagen lake
Lake Livingston
Lake Conroe
Lake Houston
DAVY CROCKETT NATIONAL FOREST
ANGELINA NATIONAL FOREST
SABINE NATIONAL FOREST
SAM HOUSTON NATIONAL FOREST
Alabama and Coushatta Indian Reservation
Apple Springs
Wells
Pollok
Burke
Etoile
Broaddus
Zavalla
Bronson
Rosevine
Geneva
Milam
Pattoon
Weches
Ratcliff
Latexo
Austonio
Midway
Cottonwood
Crabb Prairie
Riverside
Country Campus
Pointblank
Coldspring
Evergreen
New Waverly
Willis
Fostoria
Shepherd
Goodrich
Leggett
Moscow
Carmona
Woodlake
Chester
Colmesneil
Doucette
Hillister
Warren
Village Mills
Votaw
Rye
Romayor
Moss Hill
Splendora
New Caney
Porter
Spring
Dobbin
Montgomery
Plantersville
Stoneham
Anderson
Roans Prairie
Shiro
Singleton
Carlos
Bedias

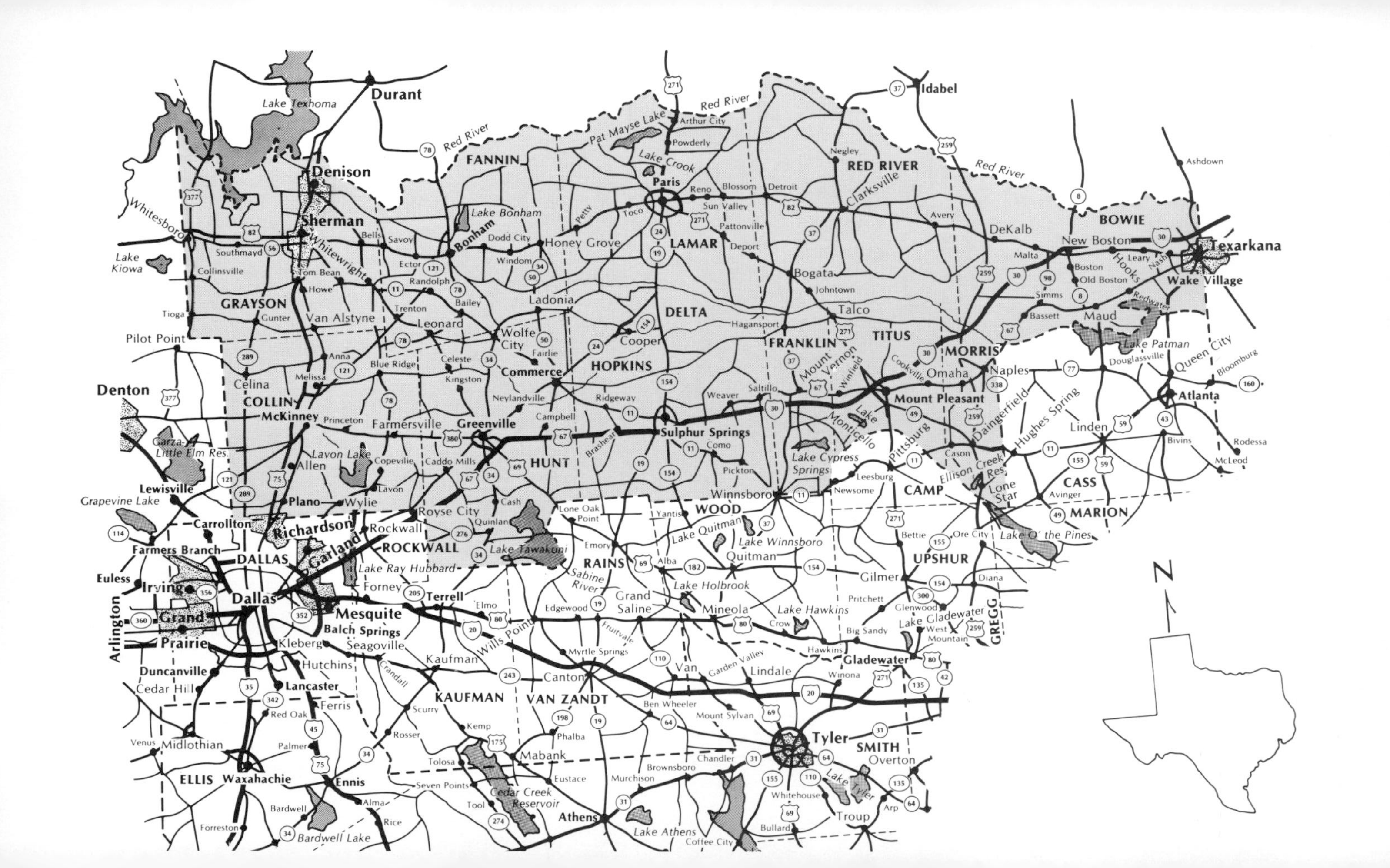

Durant
Idabel
Lake Texhoma
Red River
Denison
Sherman
Whitesboro
Lake Kiowa
FANNIN
Bonham
Lake Bonham
Honey Grove
Paris
Lake Crook
Pat Mayse Lake
Arthur City
Powderly
LAMAR
RED RIVER
Clarksville
Negley
Detroit
Blossom
Reno
BOWIE
DeKalb
New Boston
Texarkana
Wake Village
Ashdown
Hooks
Nash
Leary
Maud
Redwater
Lake Patman
Queen City
Bloomburg
Atlanta
Douglassville
GRAYSON
Gunter
Van Alstyne
Whitewright
Tom Bean
Howe
Southmayd
Collinsville
Tioga
Pilot Point
Denton
Celina
COLLIN
McKinney
Princeton
Farmersville
Greenville
Commerce
HOPKINS
DELTA
Cooper
Sulphur Springs
FRANKLIN
Mount Vernon
TITUS
Mount Pleasant
MORRIS
Naples
Omaha
Daingerfield
Hughes Spring
Linden
CASS
MARION
Lake O' the Pines
CAMP
Pittsburg
Lake Cypress Springs
Winnsboro
WOOD
Quitman
Lake Winnsboro
Mineola
Lake Holbrook
Lake Hawkins
UPSHUR
Gilmer
GREGG
Gladewater
Lake Gladewater
HUNT
Royse City
Rockwall
ROCKWALL
Lake Tawakoni
Lake Ray Hubbard
RAINS
Emory
Sabine River
Grand Saline
Wills Point
Terrell
Forney
Mesquite
Balch Springs
Garland
Richardson
Plano
Wylie
Allen
Lavon Lake
Carrollton
DALLAS
Dallas
Farmers Branch
Irving
Grand Prairie
Arlington
Euless
Grapevine Lake
Lewisville
Garza-Little Elm Res.
Duncanville
Cedar Hill
Lancaster
Hutchins
Seagoville
Kaufman
KAUFMAN
Canton
VAN ZANDT
Van
Lindale
Tyler
SMITH
Overton
Lake Tyler
Troup
Whitehouse
Bullard
Chandler
Brownsboro
Athens
Lake Athens
Cedar Creek Reservoir
Mabank
Kemp
Ennis
ELLIS
Waxahachie
Midlothian
Venus
Ferris
Bardwell Lake
Forreston
Rice
Alma
Palmer
Red Oak
Coffee City

The Red River Country

Grayson, Fannin, Lamar, Red River, Bowie, Morris, Titus, Franklin, Delta, Hopkins, Hunt and Collin Counties

This has always been border country. The border between the state of Oklahoma and the state of Texas has been peaceful now for a long time.

But at different times in history, the Red River has been the dividing line between French territory and Spanish territory, and between United States territory and Mexican territory, between Indian country and the Republic of Texas, and between Union territory and the Confederacy.

Jesse James may have spent some time here. His brother, Frank, certainly did. Belle Starr grew up here. Quantrill's Raiders had their winter base here.

Anglo settlement did not begin in this border area quite as early as it did along the eastern border. But many of the early settlers of Texas came in by fording the Red River or using the primitive ferries. The area always has been conscious of history, and several of the cities and counties here are named for heroes of the Revolution. The First Congress of the Republic established in 1836 a huge county on the border and called it Red River County. The original Red River County included all the counties in the area we have labeled Red River Country.

GRAYSON COUNTY

Interstate 45 becomes U.S. 75 after it leaves Dallas going north toward the Red River. The two biggest cities between Dallas and the Oklahoma line are both in Grayson County.

1

2

1) French tourists might be surprised to find that a century ago Texas grapes saved the French wine business from disaster. These grapes grown at the Grayson County College are descended from those raised here by T. V. Munson in the 1870s. Cuttings from Munson's grapes were used in France to develop grapes resistant to a disease that was killing the French vines. 2) Munson's home, built in 1887, is now a state historic landmark.

3

3) William Clarke Quantrill became a familiar name to Grayson County residents during the Civil War. He was an outlaw by Union standards but Quantrill got sanctuary near Sherman between raids. He helped stop cattle rustling across the Red River and also managed to persuade unhappy Sherman war widows not to storm a Confederate food depot. 4) Birthplace of Dwight Eisenhower, in Denison, is one of the state's historic homes. It is open to the public. The former president was born here in 1890.

4

Grayson County was organized formally in 1846. It was named for Peter Grayson. He was Attorney General of the Republic of Texas. Sherman has been the county seat from the beginning. The Handbook of Texas says the first courthouse was torn down in 1858 in order to settle an argument over whether there was a grey goose nesting under the building. The Handbook does not say whether a goose nest was found. The next courthouse was burned by a mob in 1930 during one of the last race riots in Texas. The present Grayson County Courthouse at Sherman was built in 1935.

1

1) The Grayson County Courthouse in Sherman was built in 1935 to replace an older courthouse burned by a mob in 1930. Sherman was called "The Athens of Texas" because it had a dramatic club as early as 1860 and an unusual number of colleges began there in the 19th Century.

The first Europeans to visit this area were French explorers. They found Caddo Indians living here. The Anglo settlers began moving in about 1835. The first settlement grew up around Abel Warren's trading post in 1836 about where Pilot Grove is today. Holland Coffee established a trading post at Preston Bend in 1837. There is a marker at the site, 8 miles north of Pottsboro, on Farm Road 120.

The first steamboat came up the Red River to the Grayson County area in 1856, and Sherman became a stop on the Butterfield Stage route from St. Louis to California in 1858.

A pioneer cottonseed mill established in Sherman in the 1870's is still in business making Mrs. Tucker's Shortening at 1201 E. Pecan. Anderson-Clayton Foods now owns the plant. No one named Mrs. Tucker ever was connected with it.

The oldest surviving house in Grayson County is the Thompson home at 1200 East Main Street in Sherman.

Denison was another early stop on the Butterfield Stage Line. The line entered Texas at Colbert's Ferry on the Red River five miles north of Denison. The ferry was established in 1853 by a Cherokee Indian named Ben Colbert. He got very rich, and it's been rumored for years that he buried a lot of money somewhere around the ferry landing. If anyone has found it, he has not said anything about it. Traffic has been crossing the Red River by bridge here since 1931.

Denison became a major railroad center during the heyday of the railroads, and Dwight Eisenhower was born into a railroading family here on October 14, 1890. The birthplace of the late president is now a museum. It is open every day,

2

2) Benjamin F. Colbert is buried here. He was a Cherokee Indian, and he made a lot of money running a ferry across the Red River near Denison just before the Civil War. The ferry was not replaced by a bridge until 1931. Ben Colbert died long before that. Rumors circulated that Colbert had buried some of his wealth nearby, so the present owner put up the stone wall to keep treasure hunters out.

and there is a small admission charge. The Eisenhower house is on South Lamar at Day in Denison.

The state has put a marker on the home of Thomas Volney Munson at 530 West Hanna Street in Denison because of the work he did with grapevines in this country. Munson came here from Kentucky in 1876. He had been growing grapes in Kentucky. He brought some cuttings here with him and began crossing them with the wild grapes he found growing along the creeks in Grayson County. Munson developed hundreds of varieties. And he may have saved the wine industry in France by sending French grape growers some of his hybrid vines during a crisis when the French vines were being attacked by a disease they were not able to withstand. The French growers crossed the Grayson County vines with their own and saved their vineyards. The government of France gave Munson the Legion of Honor. And the Grayson County College at Denison is still growing some of the grapes T. V. Munson developed.

The Whitewright Museum at Bond and Grand in Whitewright features local memorabilia and artifacts from the old Grayson College Museum. The Whitewright Museum is open afternoons, Mondays through Saturdays, and there is no admission charge.

The Van Alstyne Museum at 212 Jefferson Street in Van Alstyne features historical items and a general store and a toy collection. It is open weekdays, 10 a.m. to 2 p.m. and is free.

Lake Texoma lies along the northwestern corner of Grayson County. It is one of the biggest artificial lakes in the country and very popular with water sports enthusiasts.

1) The Denison Dam impounds the Red River a short distance below the junction of the Red and Washita Rivers. The dam forms the largest lake lying wholly or partly in Texas. Only nine other reservoirs in the United States have a greater capacity. Salt springs along the border between Texas and Oklahoma give portions of the river a saline content which limits its usefulness. But fishing is considered excellent in the lake.

Eisenhower State Park is on the lake seven miles northwest of Denison. The park covers more than 450 acres, and there is a marina with provisions for camping, swimming and fishing. This is one of the State's Class I parks, and the admission free is $1.00 per vehicle unless you have an annual permit or a State Parklands' passport. The park is off Farm Road 1310.

Camping is also allowed in the Hagerman National Wildlife Refuge 15 miles west of Denison on Lake Texoma. The refuge covers more than 11,000 acres. Boating and fishing are permitted in the refuge during the summer months.

William Clarke Quantrill was practicing during the Civil War a method of fighting that would later be termed Commando tactics. Quantrill and a small band of irregulars specialized in striking behind Union lines and causing commotion and confusion. He captured the Missouri town of Independence in 1862, and carried out repeated raids in Kansas, Missouri and Kentucky, during 1863 and 1864. Quantrill and his raiders came to Texas to do their resting and regrouping between raids. Their Texas camp was outside Sherman at a place they called Kentuckytown. Quantrill died in Kentucky in 1865 after being shot during a raid near Taylorsville. And there is not much left of Kentuckytown today except the old Baptist Church about midway between Tom Bean and Whitewright on State Highway 11.

2

3

2) The Fannin County Courthouse is one of the newer ones in Texas. It was built in 1965. But this is not where the county seat began. Two earlier locations didn't work out and the county headquarters moved to the town of Bonham in 1845, when Texas joined the Union. 3) Bonham developed from the settlement that began with this log fort (left) called Fort Inglish. In 1843, the town was named for Alamo hero James Bonham. The old fort gives an idea of the protection settlers felt they needed on the Texas frontier.

FANNIN COUNTY

Fannin County was organized in 1838. The county was named for Colonel James Fannin. He was in command of a small force of Texans executed near Goliad after they surrendered to the Mexican Army in 1836. Fannin is ranked with the heroes of the Revolution. The history books seldom mention that he was a slave trader at Velasco before the Revolution. Fannin was born in Georgia. He came to Texas in 1834. He apparently never was anywhere near the county that now bears his name.

The county seat of Fannin County is named for another hero of the Revolution. James Butler Bonham was a classmate and close friend of William Barret Travis back in South Carolina. Travis invited Bonham to Texas in 1835, and Bonham became part of Travis' outnumbered force at the Alamo. Bonham had a chance to save himself because Travis

1

1) This reminder of an earlier era is the John Milt Nunn house in Bonham, at 505 W. 5th St. It carries the state's historic medallion, but it is not open to the public.

sent him out twice to try to organize a relief expedition. Bonham was not able to get any help, but he slipped through the Mexican lines back into the Alamo both times. He was there to be killed along with the rest of the defenders on March 6, 1836. Bonham never was near here, either, but his statue stands on the courthouse square. The present courthouse was built in 1965, and it includes part of an older courthouse built in 1888.

Bonham is not the oldest town in the county, and it was not the original county seat. Two settlements were established here in 1836. A small party of settlers established a place they called Lexington, and Abel Warren established a trading post he called Fort Warren. Both were on the Red River. Lexington was the first county seat when Fannin County was organized. The settlement changed its name to Tulip and then died after the county government moved to Fort Warren in 1840. Fort Warren apparently was a place like you might see in a movie. It had a wall of logs around it with watch towers at the corners. Fort Warren lasted long enough to become known as Old Warren. But it died after the county government moved away in 1845. Bonham became the county seat that year, and the county government has been here ever since.

Bonham grew up around a log fort Bailey Inglish built on Powder Creek in 1837. The settlement was called Bois d'Arc until they decided in 1843 to name it for James Bonham.

The most famous citizen of Fannin County and Bonham was Sam Rayburn. The home the late Speaker of the U.S. House of Representatives occupied is preserved as a museum. The home is about one and one-half miles west of Bonham on U.S. Highway 82. It is open weekdays except Mondays. There is no charge. The Sam Rayburn Library is in downtown Bonham, on U.S. 82. It houses the Speaker's official papers and a replica of the office he occupied in the Capitol during

2

3

2) Sam Rayburn is well-remembered in Fannin County. His home, above, just west of Bonham, has become a museum. 3) And the Rayburn library, in downtown Bonham, commemorates and preserves the former House Speaker's career and papers.

the years he was the second most powerful man in Washington. Former President Harry Truman came to Bonham to help dedicate the Rayburn Library in 1957. The library is open every day and free.

There is another Class I State Park in this county. The Bonham State Park on Lake Bonham, four miles outside the city of Bonham, has provisions for camping and swimming and boating. There are paddle boats for rent. The entrance fee is $1.00 per vehicle unless you have the annual permit. This permit can be obtained from the Texas Parks and Wildlife Department in Austin and at park entrances for $15.00 a year. It entitles you to unlimited use of the state parks for 12 months.

Part of the Caddo-Lyndon B. Johnson National Grassland Reserve is in Fannin County. This is land the Federal Govern-

1

1) Another of Fannin County's preserved, historic homes is the W. W. Brownlee place at 220 W. 6th St. in Fannin. It illustrates the elegance and the gingerbread touches that many successful Texans affected in the Victorian period. The Brownlee home is not open to the public.

ment bought up after the disastrous drought of the 1930's. The extensive plowing and cultivation of land in the middle west aggravated the dust storms during that period. The lands bought up under the National Grassland Reserve program have been allowed to go back to native grasses and brush so there will be less dust to blow next time.

Any list of comical place names always includes the name of Bug Tussle, in southeastern Fannin County. There is not much to see here, but if you want to be able to say you've been to Bug Tussle, you can find it between Honey Grove and Ladonia where Highway 34 and Farm Road 1550 meet.

LAMAR COUNTY

Lamar County was created in 1840. It was named for Mirabeau B. Lamar. He was the first Vice President and the second President of the Republic of Texas.

The county seat is Paris. It grew from a settlement originally called Pinhook, and it became the county seat in 1844 when original settler George Wright donated 50 acres for the townsite.

The county government previously had more or less camped out at a settlement called Lafayette and at another settlement called Mount Vernon. The people here seem to have favored grand names from the beginning. An ornate granite courthouse was destroyed by fire here in 1916. The present courthouse was built in 1917.

2

3

4

2) Samuel Bell Maxey thought his fighting days were over when he moved to Lamar County after the Mexican War. But his law career was interrupted by the Civil War and he formed the Ninth Texas Regiment to fight for the Confederacy. 3) Maxey's home in Paris is now a Texas historic landmark and it is open to visitors. 4) When the Lamar County Courthouse was built in 1917, it was obviously built to last. Much civic pride is evident in the design and proportions of this granite monument. The jail was included on the top floor.

Lamar County was one of the Texas counties siding with Sam Houston against seceding from the Union in 1860. The vote was 553 in favor and 663 against joining the Confederacy. Union sympathy never died completely, but the county gave substantial support to the Confederate cause. Cattleman John Chisum supplied beef for the Confederate armies throughout the war.

Samuel Bell Maxey recruited the Ninth Texas Regiment for the Confederacy from Lamar and surrounding counties. Maxey was a veteran of the Mexican War. He moved to Texas from Kentucky after that war, and he was practicing law in Paris when the Civil War began. Maxey rose to the rank of major general in the Confederate Army and returned to Paris at the end of the war. He was elected to the United States Senate after Reconstruction. He died in 1895, and he is buried in Evergreen Cemetery in Paris. His home at 812 Church Street is preserved and open to visitors Tuesdays through

1 *1) John Chisum was an entrepreneur of great imagination. He helped form and manage the largest cattle outfit in North Texas prior to the Civil War. He delivered beef on the hoof to Confederate forces in the Southwest at $40 a head. He made a fortune when war came. 2) Chisum's monumental family tombstone in Paris suggests both his reputation and affluence.* 2

Saturdays and on Sunday afternoons. There is a small admission charge.

John Chisum was a character designed to be played by John Wayne. He came to Texas with his parents when he was 13, and they settled in the community that is now Paris. He built the first county courthouse and served a term as county clerk before he went into the cattle business. Chisum was the biggest cattle rancher in northern Texas by the time the Civil War began. He was a beef contractor for the Confederate Army. He survived the economic debacle that followed the collapse of the Confederacy because he was putting the receipts for his cattle directly into more cattle as fast as the money came in. So he had a lot of cattle and very little Confederate money when the Confederate money became worthless. Chisum cut the ears of his cows in a distinctive way for identification. The cut left part of the ear dangling, and the dangling part of the ear was called a jinglebob. John Chisum became known as "Jinglebob John." He moved his cattle operations to West Texas and New Mexico after the war. His cows were driven to various markets over various trails, and some of the trails were referred to as Chisum's Trails. But these trails should not be confused with the more famous Chisholm Trail. The Chisholm Trail was named for Indian Trader Jesse Chisholm. He was not a cattleman, and he was not a trail driver. But he blazed the original trail from the Oklahoma territory to Wichita, Kansas. That trail and the

3

4

3) Henry W. Lightfoot was a noted Paris lawyer in the 1870s and a partner of General Sam Bell Maxey. The old Lightfoot house in Paris is restored to its original condition and may be visited by appointment. 4) Belle Starr was one of the state's early outlaws. She was hardly a local favorite but she was rather well-known in Paris. Belle was an occupant of the local jail briefly before she was killed in 1889.

various extensions of it all the way down into south Texas have been known ever since as the Chisholm Trail. John Chisum died in Arkansas in 1884 at the age of 60. He is buried in Paris, at Washington Street and the Santa Fe tracks.

The Lightfoot house in Paris is a typical early Texas ranch home, and it is shown to visitors by appointment. The Lightfoot house is at 746 Church Street.

Belle Starr is supposed to have spent a little time in jail here in Paris. Belle was born Myra Belle Shirley in Missouri in 1848. She moved to East Texas with her parents in 1856 and got in with the wrong crowd. She eloped with an outlaw named Reed and then married a Cherokee hoodlum named Sam Starr after Reed was killed by lawmen. Sam and Belle carried on a career in horse thievery and general crime until he

1

2

1) The old time general stores are not all gone yet. Top photo shows the one still operating at Roxton in Lamar County. The Nettie Whipple General Store is alive and well — and selling merchandise new as well as old. 2) World War II veterans and their descendants can examine aviation relics of that era at the Flying Tiger Museum near Paris. A vintage A-20 and a B-25 are among the prizes here.

was killed in a gunfight in 1886. She was shot to death in Oklahoma in 1889.

The Flying Tiger Museum on U.S. Highway 82, two miles west of Paris, is a collection of old airplanes. Most of them are from World War II. There is no fee.

There are provisions for camping and boating and fishing at Lake Crook, three miles northwest of Paris, and also at the Pat Mayse Reservoir, 13 miles north of Paris, off U.S. 271.

The Gambill Goose Sanctuary on Farm Road 79 at Farm Road 2820 northwest of Paris is a refuge for geese traveling

3

3) Red River County is named for the long, meandering river that separates Texas and Oklahoma before it turns south to snake its way to the Mississippi. From source to mouth, the Red is about 1,360 miles long. The River forms the northern boundary of Texas for 640 of these miles.

between Texas and Canada. It was started by a farmer named John Gambill out of his own interest in the migrating geese. Gambill put out food for the geese every year for 35 years, and they made his farm a regular stop. The state is carrying the operation on now. Feeding time at the Gambill Goose Sanctuary is 4:00 every afternoon, from the middle of October to the middle of March. The refuge is on Lake Gibbons, 10 miles northwest of Paris.

RED RIVER COUNTY

Red River County takes its name from the river, and the river takes its name from the color of the soil it carries along from the Texas Panhandle and empties into the Mississippi north of Baton Rouge.

The Caddo Indians were living here long before the first European explorers came. They were peaceful farmers, and they eventually allowed themselves to be hustled off to reservations. There were some Kickapoo, Shawnees and Delawares living here, too, by the time the first Anglo settlers came about 1814. The Kickapoos, Shawnees and Delawares came here from the eastern United States to get out of the way of the white settlers there. They were driven out of Texas along with the Cherokees during the days of the Republic in an exercise described in later chapters. Two Caddo mounds in this county are listed in the National Register of Historical Places, but both are on private property. The county seat was

1

1) Not too many of the imposing 19th Century courthouses remain standing in Texas, in anything like mint condition. This Red River County Courthouse at Clarksville is one survivor and among the oldest. It was erected in 1885, when the community had half a dozen churches, a Catholic convent, three schools, two banks and two flour mills. The county today is still largely involved with agribusiness as it was when the courthouse went up.

put at a settlement called LaGrange when the county was first organized. But it was moved a short time later to Clarksville, and it has been in Clarksville ever since.

Clarksville was established in 1833 by James Clark. The town never grew very large, but it was the site of several early schools. The Clarksville Academy, the Clarksville Male and Female Academy and the McKenzie College all operated in or near here in the early 1840's. The present courthouse in Clarksville was built in 1885. It is one of the older courthouses in the State. Some of the older courthouses have been remodeled and modernized. But the State has taken an interest in preserving the character of the remaining old courthouses, and county governments now must give the Texas Historical Commission six months notice before they make any structural changes in a courthouse. The notice gives the Commission time to take some action if it determines the changes will damage the historical value of the building. Some unfortunate remodeling projects could have been prevented if the State had taken this action earlier. But better late than never.

One of the early Texas newspapers was founded in Clarksville by Charles DeMorse. He came to Texas from Massachusetts to fight in the revolution. He arrived a bit too late to take part in the fighting, but he served some time in the Texas Navy and the Texas Army before he started practicing law at Matagorda. DeMorse moved to Clarksville in 1842 and founded the *Northern Standard.* He had a career in politics,

2) Charles DeMorse is often called the father of Texas journalism. He built this home when he moved to Clarksville in the 1840s. It began as two log rooms and grew into what was then considered a palatial residence. It continued to be occupied by DeMorse descendants well into the 20th Century. 3) Another of Clarksville's historic homes is the W. L. Nunnely home at 507 Locust.

3

too, and he fought in the Civil War on the Confederate side. But he continued to be listed as editor and publisher of the *Northern Standard* until he died in 1887. He is considered the father of Texas journalism. There is a marker at the site of the original office of the *Northern Standard,* and one at the DeMorse home. The office was at 313 North Locust Street. The home is at 115 East Comanche.

A marker on Farm Road 410, 17 miles northwest of Clarksville, proclaims that Sam Houston first set foot on the soil of Texas near here in December of 1832. Houston came here originally as an agent of President Andrew Jackson and the

1

1) The nation's 32nd vice president was born in Red River County in 1868. John Nance Garner lived the early part of his life in and around Detroit, Texas, earning his first spending money as a shortstop for the Coon Soup Hollow Blossom Prairie baseball team. He was one of only two men ever to be both House speaker and Vice President and he was one of the first to advance the idea that the federal government should insure bank deposits. Garner and his parents lived for a time in the house 2) at Detroit which is now marked as an historical home. Garner died in 1967, just short of his 99th birthday. Some historians contend that Garner paved the way for other prominent Texans to reach high national office.

2

3

3) Some Texas counties did not support secession prior to the Civil War, but nearly all did wind up sending troops to fight for the Confederacy. Many counties around the state put up monuments like this after the Union occupation ended in the 1870s. This monument commemorates the 10 companies of men Red River County sent to fight for the Confederacy. The monument is in Clarksville.

Cherokee Indians. His career is described in more detail in the chapter on Walker County.

There is a marker on Farm Road 410, six miles northwest of Detroit, where John Nance Garner was born. There is another marker at 200 South Main Street in Detroit, where Garner and his parents lived for a time. Garner was Vice President of the United States during President Franklin D. Roosevelt's first two terms, from 1932 to 1940.

BOWIE COUNTY

Boston, the county seat of Bowie County, is not the principal city. And the principal city is largely in another state.

The principal city is Texarkana. It is at the northeastern edge of Texas, and a good part of the city is in the state of Arkansas. It is actually two cities. There is a separate city government for the part in Texas and a separate city government for the part in Arkansas. The two cities share the same Federal Building. It is on the state line, half in Texas and half in Arkansas.

This was Caddo country, too. There are more than 70 Caddo mounds in the county. Bowie County was formed in 1840. It was named for the Alamo hero James Bowie. He was a smuggler and slave trader in Louisiana before he came to Texas and threw in with the forces agitating for separation from Mexico. Bowie took part in the capture of San Antonio

1

1) Alamo hero James Bowie had a knife named for him. A North Texas county was named for him, too. But he did not live here. He was an adventurer of many interests when he came to Texas in 1828 to settle. Bowie was ill when the Alamo fell but he was said to have died fighting there. 2) This monument to Bowie was erected by the State of Texas at Texarkana in 1936.

2

in 1835, and he was in command of the irregular forces there when Santa Anna took it back in 1836. He was killed with the rest of the garrison. There is a monument to James Bowie at 901 State Line Avenue in Texarkana. He never was here. But Ben Milam was.

Ben Milam is listed as the first Anglo settler in what is now Bowie County. He apparently was the first to discover that small steamboats could travel this far up the Red River by maneuvering around and through the rafts of logs and drift-

3) Bowie County is unusual in that the county seat of Boston is a tiny town and its largest city is divided between two states. It takes some municipal cooperation for Texarkana to co-exist in Arkansas and Texas. As the photo shows, the two Texarkanas share the same federal building situated right on the state line. Texarkana developed partly because it was on the Great Southwest Trail the earliest Indians used in traveling from tribal lands in Mississippi to the Caddo lands of northeast Texas. Railroads and then highways later followed much the same route.

wood clogging the stream. The rafts and logjams in the river channel created back channels and byways that knowledgeable skippers could navigate. Ports grew up on the Red River and at Jefferson on Caddo Lake as a result. Settlers and the U.S. Army Engineers thought if all the obstructions were removed, the Red River would be a great avenue of commerce. The engineers worked off and on for more than 30 years to clear the rafts and logjams. They succeeded. But the result was not what they had hoped. The cleared channel allowed water to drain into the Mississippi faster and the water level in the Red River dropped so low that navigation was possible only during floods. The principal casualty was the Port of Jefferson. More about that in the chapter on Marion County

Ben Milam came to this part of the world to trade with the Indians. That was in 1818. He came across a band of Comanches David Burnet happened to be living with, and he and Burnet became close friends. Burnet had been hurt in a fall from a horse, and the Comanches had taken him in. Burnet went on to become President of the interim government of Texas. But Ben Milam did not live to see that happen. Milam was in Mexico on business for empresario Arthur Wavell when the Mexican General Martin Perfecto de Cos marched into Texas to put an end to the settlers' agitation for independence. Milam was captured by Cos' troops as he was returning to Texas. He escaped and joined the Texas force gearing up to oppose the Cos expedition. Milam was killed in

1) Ben Milam came to Texas in 1818 and helped to explore and settle the area that is now Bowie County. He thought the Red River would be a major trade artery like the Mississippi but it never was. Milam made friends with the Indians and later joined the Texas independence movement. He played a leading role in the attack on Mexican forces in San Antonio, where he was killed. 2) Memorabilia from the settling of northeast Texas may be seen at the Texarkana Historical Museum.

the battle where the Texans captured San Antonio and General Cos. That battle provoked Santa Anna's 1836 expedition into Texas.

The county seat of the county they named for Jim Bowie after Ben Milam settled it is Boston. The original settlement of this name grew up around a store established by W. J. Boston. It was discovered later that Boston was a little short of being within five miles of the center of the county as a

3) The courthouse at Boston, county seat of Bowie County, represents a quirk of history. An early Texas law required that county seats be within five miles of the center of the county. So early settlers found they were in the wrong place. They moved — then moved again when the railroad came through. Three Bostons resulted. The one with the courthouse is one of the smallest county seats in Texas. 4) This bust of Scott Joplin in the Texarkana museum honors one of Bowie County's most famous sons. The great ragtime composer died in 1917.

county seat was supposed to be. So some of the residents and the county government moved closer to the center of the county and started a new settlement named Boston. The original Boston became known as Old Boston. The first railroad came through a little later. It passed a little north of Boston, and a new settlement grew up there beside the tracks. It is called New Boston. The county government stayed at Boston. It is a very small town. The present courthouse was built in 1889.

There is no marker to show where Ben Milam lived, but he surely spent some time at the Arthur Wavell Colony because

1

1) The Draughn-Moore house is also called the "Ace of Clubs" house because its design resembles the three leaves and stem of a "club." The house was built in 1883 by a prominent early merchant. It is a private residence today, but it may ultimately become the property of the Texarkana Historical Society. This Italianate structure is the lone survivor of 19th Century residential architecture near downtown Texarkana. The location is 420 Pine St.

he worked for Wavell for a while. A marker off Interstate 30 near North State Line Avenue proclaims this as the site of the Wavell Colony.

A marker in Spring Lake Park declares that part of the Hernando DeSoto expedition camped here in the 16th Century

The only man ever to win an election over Sam Houston came from here. Hardin Runnels beat Houston for the governor's office in 1857, but he lost the re-match in 1859. The old Runnels home is at 1402 W. 9th Street.

The Texarkana Historical Society operates a museum in the city's oldest brick building at 219 State Line Avenue. The museum is open every day, and there is no admission charge.

The U.S. Army's Red River Depot here sprawls over 50 square miles. The depot repairs and stores and maintains all kinds of equipment for Army units all over the world. The depot is on U.S. 82 between Boston and Texarkana.

Lake Wright Patman lies along the southern boundary of Bowie County. It was called Lake Texarkana until the name was changed to honor the late member of Congress. There is a Class I State Park on the lake. It is Atlanta State Park on the south bank, in Cass County. There is the usual charge of $1.00 per vehicle unless you have an annual permit or the State Parklands Passport. The passport is issued free to citizens over the age of 65. It must be applied for in person at any park entrance or at the offices of the State Department of

2

2) Hardin Runnels was active in early Texas politics. He served as House Speaker of the Fifth Legislature. He won his chief fame by beating Sam Houston for governor in 1857. Two years later Houston won the governorship by about the same margin he'd lost earlier. Runnels was one of the founders of the Texas Historical Society in 1870. 3) This is the Ned Walker house, north of Daingerfield on SH 144, off US 259. It was built in 1859. It is not open to the public.

3

Parks and Wildlife, Room 180, John Reagan Building, Austin.

MORRIS COUNTY

Morris County was established in 1875. The county apparently was named for W. W. Morris. He was a member of the legislature and a District Judge in Rusk County.

The county seat is Daingerfield. The present courthouse was built in 1971. The Morris County Museum opened in January 1978 in the old Morris County courthouse built in 1881. It has displays of Indian artifacts, old implements and utensils and furniture. The museum is open only on weekends, but it may be open weekdays a little later. There is a small fee.

There is some farming and ranching in Morris County and some commercial timber. But steel is the biggest business. There is iron ore here. The government started a steel mill

1) The business of Morris County is run from the old courthouse at Daingerfield. Settlers began arriving here in the 1840s but it wasn't until World War II that the county's iron ore deposits began to have an impact on the local economy.

during World War II. It was sold to private interests after the war, and it is now the Lone Star Steel Company. The plant uses iron ore from the immediate vicinity. The mill is south of Daingerfield on U.S. 259.

The Daingerfield State Park is two miles east of Daingerfield off State Highway 11. This is a Class I Park, covering 600 acres. There is a lake with boat ramps and a fishing pier. There are cabins and provisions for camping and hiking. There is an admission fee of $1.00 per vehicle unless you have an annual permit, and the cabin fees are in addition to that. You can reserve cabins in the Daingerfield State Park by writing to Post Office Box "B", Daingerfield, Texas 75638, or by phoning 214-645-2921.

The northern tip of Lake O' The Pines reaches into the southern end of Morris County, near Lone Star. Most of the lake, though, is in Marion County.

This area was represented in Congress for many years by members of the Sheppard family. Morris Sheppard was elected to the U.S. House of Representatives in 1902, to succeed his late father John Sheppard. Morris Sheppard served in the House until he was elected to the Senate in 1913. Senator Sheppard introduced the bill that became the 18th

2) Simplicity and a big front porch were uppermost in the builder's mind when the Walker House was erected at Naples, in Morris County, in the 1850s. 2

Amendment to the Constitution of the United States. That was the amendment that brought on prohibition, and Sheppard also collaborated with Andrew Volstead in drafting the Volstead Act to enforce the amendment. The nation later changed its mind about prohibition, but Morris Sheppard never did. He was a member of the U.S. Senate and a prohibitionist until he died in 1941.

TITUS COUNTY

Titus County was organized in 1846. It was named for early settler A. J. Titus. He came to Texas from Tennessee in 1838. He fought in the Mexican War and served in the Legislature.

The town of Mount Pleasant was established to be the county seat when the county was organized, and it has been the county seat ever since. The present county courthouse was built in 1895. The name supposedly was chosen just because the location is such a pleasant spot.

There was here one of those mineral springs people used to gather around before automobiles and movies and television. It was a flourishing resort from about 1908 to about 1915. The site of the resort is now Dellwood Park, about one mile south of the square in Mount Pleasant.

Among the buildings with historical markers in this county are the Lide House at 422 East Third Street in Mount Pleas-

1

1) A relatively new county courthouse sits in the middle of the town square at Mount Pleasant, seat of Titus County. This is a retail center for several surrounding counties. The county's marketable timber has declined, but manufacturing in Mount Pleasant is increasing. 2) The Lide House at Mount Pleasant and 3) The Slaughter House, six miles north of Mount Pleasant, are examples of 19th Century homes that have been maintained to the present day.

2

3

4) Franklin County's Courthouse was clearly designed in the grand tradition of the early Texas courthouse builders, complete with cupola and clock with four faces. Oil has brought changes to the county but the population is about the same as it was a century ago. 4

ant and the W. A. Keith House on U.S. 67 at Cookville. These houses are not open to the public.

FRANKLIN COUNTY

Franklin County was organized in 1875. It was named in honor of B. C. Franklin. He was one of the veterans of the Battle of San Jacinto. He came to Texas from Georgia to fight in the revolution. He was the first man appointed to be a District Judge in the Republic of Texas. He spent most of his life and did most of his work in Galveston and Brazoria Counties. He never was anywhere near Franklin County, and he died two years before the county was established.

The county seat of Franklin County is Mount Vernon on Interstate 30 in the center of the county. The present courthouse in Mount Vernon was built in 1912. The town of Mount Vernon grew out of a settlement originally named Lone Star.

The woods along State Highway 37 and Farm Road 21 in

1

1) Mount Vernon's first physician was William C. Wright. He built this home about 1870 and it was occupied by his descendants for a century. It is called the Wright-Vaughn House and it has been restored by its present owners. 2) The A. J. Drummond home is located near Hopewell, southeast of Mount Vernon on FM 21.

2

the southern part of Franklin County make a colorful show in the fall.

Buildings with historical markers in the county include the Rutherford Drug Store at 101 Houston Street in Mount Vernon and the Wright-Vaughn House at 110 W. Main Street in Mount Vernon. Football player and commentator Don Meredith was born in Mount Vernon.

DELTA COUNTY

Delta County was organized in 1870. The name supposedly was chosen because the county has a triangular shape resembling the Greek letter Delta. There are no mineral

3

3) There were dense woods where the Delta County Courthouse now stands when the first settlers came in 1841. Parts of the county remained a hideout for outlaws until the 1870s. 4) The George Washington Morris home, marked with the state's historical medallion and plaque, is located in Cooper, the county seat.

4

deposits of much consequence. The principal business here is farming and ranching.

Anglo settlement did not begin in this area until the 1840's. The county seat is Cooper. It was named for State Senator W. L. Cooper. The present courthouse was built in 1940.

The Patterson Memorial Library and Museum is housed in the restored Texas and Midland Railroad Depot at 700 West Dallas Street in Cooper. The museum features collections of furniture and farm implements and tools from the early days. The museum is open Friday and Saturday afternoons. There is no charge for admission.

Historical markers in the county include:

The site of Camp Rusk, one and one-half miles southwest of Ben Franklin on Road Road 128; The Thomas J. Lane

1

1) Courthouse buffs may enjoy visiting the Hopkins County Courthouse at Sulphur Springs. It was obviously influenced by the monumental and ornate building styles of the Victorian period. The county has some oil and gas production but the dairy farms are the backbone of the Hopkins County economy. There are more than 500 of them.

home, three miles southwest of Ben Franklin on Farm Road 128; The Cinderella Chapman home, one mile south of Cooper, off Liberty Grove Road; The George M. Terrell home, 341 Waco Avenue, in Cooper; The George Washington Morris home, 150 E. Waco Avenue, in Cooper.

HOPKINS COUNTY

Hopkins County was formed in 1846. It was named for a pioneer family. The town of Sulphur Springs has been the county seat since 1871. The town was originally called Bright Star. It grew up around a stop on the road wagon trains used when they were hauling freight from the river port at Jefferson to points west. The townspeople chose the name Sulphur Springs because they had some mineral springs and they were trying to ballyhoo the place as a health resort. A great many other towns were doing the same thing, and some of the others did it better. The present county courthouse was built in 1895. People traveling to Sulphur Springs had to use the stage coach from the railroad depot at Mineola until the railroad reached Sulphur Springs in 1876. The population rose to 15,000 in the 1880's. It has declined some since then.

There is some oil and gas production in Hopkins County, but the biggest business here is dairy farming. The Texas Almanac ranks Hopkins County as the number one county in the entire country in dairying.

Thomas Jefferson Rusk held one of the original land grants

2

3

2) Remains of an early settler's residence called the Atkins House are on Atkins Street in Sulphur Springs. 3) Craftsmanship on a diminutive scale is an attraction at the Hopkins County Museum in Sulphur Springs. Visitors may see more than 300 antique music boxes on exhibit here. They are from the personal collection of Leo St. Clair, and he is often on hand to demonstrate them. He collected the tiny music boxes over a period of fifty years.

in this county. But he apparently never lived here. He was a signer of the Texas Declaration of Independence and one of the leaders of the Texas Revolution.

The Hopkins County Museum is housed in the City Library in Sulphur Springs. One of the features here is a collection of more than 300 old music boxes.

Historical markers in the county include a Memorial to General W. H. King, on the courthouse grounds in Sulphur Springs, and the old Atkins House, at 126 Atkins Street in Sulphur Springs.

HUNT COUNTY

Hunt County was formed in 1846 and named for Memucan Hunt. He was Secretary of the Texas Navy in the Mirabeau Lamar Administration in the early days of the Republic.

1) The Hunt County Courthouse in Greenville is now a half century old. There was a major Indian camping ground near this site when the first Anglo settlers arrived in 1839. But the Kiowas threatened the pioneers mostly with prairie fires and thievery.

The county seat is Greenville in the center of the county. Greenville grew up around a store Ben Anderson established in 1844. The present courthouse was completed in 1928. The town was named for Thomas Green. He fought as a private at San Jacinto and as a general in the Civil War. He was killed in battle in 1864. There is oil and gas production here and some manufacturing and farming.

The North City Park in Greenville features a small zoo and a swimming pool and the home of pioneer businessman Fred Von Ende. The home is the oldest one still standing in Greenville. It has been turned into a museum featuring furniture and implements used by pioneer families in the area. The museum in the Ende-Gaillard House is open Sunday afternoons during the summer months.

There are historical markers on the old Bourland-Stevens-Samuel House at 1916 Stonewall and on the General Hal C.

2

2) Two of the oldest historic homes in Greenville are the Ende-Gaillard House, above, and 3) the Horton House. Fred Von Ende's early home has become a museum, open during the summer months. General Hal C. Horton's old home, at left, is still a private residence and is not open to the public.

3

Horton House at 3925 Moulton Street. But they are private residences and not open to the public.

A family named Horton does a big business in Christmas fruitcakes out of a shop at a place they call Puddin' Hill on the outskirts of Greenville.

A marker outside Celeste, on U.S. 69, south of Kingston, recalls that Audie Murphy was born here. Murphy was the most decorated American serviceman of World War II.

General Claire Chennault was born in Commerce, at 1501 Monroe Street. Chennault was the commander of the "Flying Tigers" volunteer air force that fought for China before Pearl Harbor.

Commerce is also the home of East Texas State University. This school was established originally as a teachers' college in 1889.

1

A number of entrepreneurs around Texas have done well in the business of making fruitcakes. The Puddin' Hill Store 1) at Greenville gets especially busy at Christmas. Visitors and customers are welcome here. 2) One of Hunt County's most distinguished sons was Major General Claire Chennault, of Flying Tigers fame. He was born in this house at Commerce in 1890. He was related to Sam Houston through his father and to Robert E. Lee through his mother.

2

Lake Tawakoni at the southern edge of the county is one of the larger lakes in the state. It covers more than 36,000 acres and has more than 200 miles of shoreline in this and two other counties. There are numerous commercial marinas, campgrounds and boat ramps around the lake but no major state park.

COLLIN COUNTY

Collin County and the county seat both were named for the same man. The county has Collin McKinney's first name, and the city of McKinney has his last name. The present Collin County Courthouse at McKinney was built in 1874 and remodeled in 1927. The county was organized in 1846. Collin McKinney's fame was well established by that time. He had

…llin County's courthouse was built more than a century ago, but it …esn't look it. The county did some modernization work in the 1920s. 3

settled here in 1831. He had represented the Red River area at the Convention at Washington-on-the-Brazos in 1836, and he was one of the signers of the Declaration of Independence drafted there. There was some uncertainty at that time whether McKinney's home place was in Arkansas or Texas. But Collin McKinney was a Texan by temperament and instinct, and he served three terms in the Texas House of Representatives before it was definitely established that his place was in Texas. McKinney died in 1861, and the house where he died was moved to Finch Park to be preserved. The park and the house are in south McKinney, off Kentucky Street.

Another early settler here was James Webb Throckmorton. He came in 1841. Throckmorton was an Army surgeon in the Mexican War and served in the Legislature. He was a delegate to the Secession Convention in 1861. He voted against seceding, but took an oath of loyalty to the Confederacy after the convention decided to secede. Throckmorton served in the Confederate forces, and he was elected Governor in the election immediately following the Civil War. He did not get to serve long. Governor Throckmorton and other elected state officials were removed from office by General Philip Sheridan. The Union Army was occupying the South. Sheridan was Military Governor of Texas and Louisiana. He accused Throckmorton and the other elected officials of hindering Reconstruction. He removed them in 1867 and

1

1) "Old Leathercoat" was the nickname hung on General James Webb Throckmorton, one of Collin County's best-known early settlers. He served in both Mexican and Civil Wars and later served a very brief, interrupted term as Texas governor. He was still trying to get reelected governor in 1890 when he developed the illness that killed him in 1894. This statue of him stands on the courthouse square in McKinney. 2) Collin McKinney's 1846 cabin has been restored to its original condition and it was moved in 1937 to this site in McKinney's Finch Park.

2

3

3) One of the more carefully restored homes of the 19th Century may be seen in Frisco, Texas, near the western edge of Collin County, on FM 720. It is the T. J. Campbell House.

arranged for the election of more agreeable officials. General Sheridan was removed from the Military Governor's office himself a little later because President Andrew Johnson thought him too high handed. But that didn't prevent Sheridan from going on to become Commander in Chief of the United States Army. Officiousness is a trait not held against generals very often. Good generals have always been scarce, and he apparently was a good general. Sheridan is credited with being the first visitor to say that he would live in hell and rent out Texas if he owned both places.

Governor Throckmorton had his law office at 111 W. Virginia Street in McKinney. There is a state marker at the site.

There is substantial farming and ranching in Collin County, but the area increasingly is a part of the Dallas complex. The Dallas suburb of Richardson is partly within Collin County.

The largest body of water in the county is Lavon Reservoir. This lake covers more than 11,000 acres, and there are several parks around it. One of the parks has some special provisions to make it easier for blind people to fish.

The Heard Natural Science Museum and Wildlife Sanctuary outside McKinney features pictures and exhibits on natural history. Guided tours of the sanctuary can be arranged by appointment, through Dr. Harold McLaughlin at 214-542-5012. The Museum is open Tuesdays through Saturdays and on Sunday afternoons. There is no admission charge.

1 *1) This vintage home at Lavon in Collin County is still occupied by descendants of the original owner. It is the Forder House, now more than 90 years old.*

The biggest town in Collin County is Plano. It is the home of the University of Plano. This city was established by members of the Peters' Colony. It was named Fillmore originally, but the name was changed after about 10 years to Plano. The Peters' Colony grew out of a land grant the Republic of Texas made in 1841 to W. S. Peters and Associates. The grant allowed Peters and Associates to keep for themselves some of the land they were to grant to colonists. The deal was that this would compensate the promoters for their trouble and expense. (They were called empresarios in those days, but they were promoters). The colonists supposedly understood this, but they began to complain about it after they settled in. They came to believe that they were being required to share *their* land with the promoters. Other colonists were not having to kick back any land. The Peters Colonists made enough commotion to cause the Legislature to change the Peters deal and give to the colonists the lands the promoters had been claiming. The Peters group threatened to go to court to get damages. The Legislature settled the thing by giving the Peters outfit a lot more land farther west. The state had more land than money and wanted more settlers. The empresarios were bringing in settlers.

2) Guy and Bunnin Brinlee take the air on the front porch of their antique home outside Blue Ridge. The Brinlee brothers welcome visitors. 2

One of the smaller communities in Collin County is Lavon on Highway 78 in the southeastern corner of the county where Mrs. Charles Forder is still living in the home her family occupied during the days when Lavon was a busy railroad town. The house and Mrs. Forder both are more than 90 years old.

Outside Blue Ridge Guy Brinlee and his brother, Bunnun Brinlee, are still living in a house built before the Civil War. The house has no more conveniences or amenities than it had when it was new. The Brinlee brothers say they don't need those things. But they are not hermits. They are glad to have visitors stop by and chat. Their old place is five miles northeast of Blue Ridge on State Highway 78.

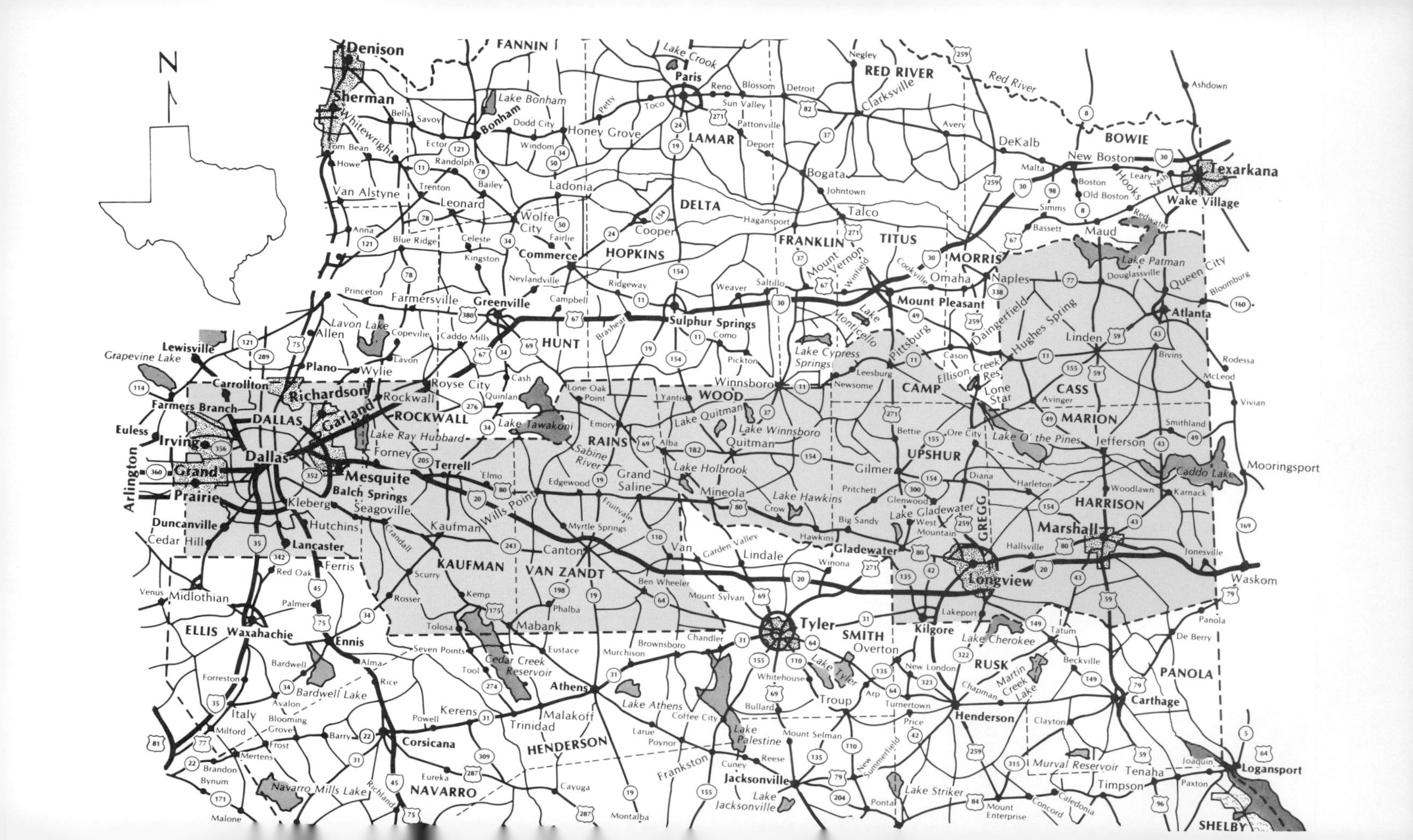

N
Denison
Sherman
Whitewright
Tom Bean
Howe
Van Alstyne
Anna
Bells
Savoy
Ector
FANNIN
Lake Bonham
Bonham
Dodd City
Windom
Honey Grove
Petty
Toco
Lake Crook
Paris
Reno
Blossom
Sun Valley
Pattonville
Detroit
Deport
LAMAR
Negley
RED RIVER
Clarksville
Red River
Avery
DeKalb
BOWIE
New Boston
Malta
Boston
Old Boston
Hooks
Leary
Nash
Texarkana
Wake Village
Ashdown
Simms
Bassett
Maud
Redwater
Randolph
Trenton
Bailey
Leonard
Ladonia
Wolfe City
Fairlie
Celeste
Blue Ridge
Kingston
Commerce
Neylandville
DELTA
Cooper
HOPKINS
Hagansport
Bogata
Johntown
Talco
FRANKLIN
TITUS
Mount Vernon
Winfield
Cookville
Omaha
MORRIS
Naples
Lake Patman
Douglassville
Queen City
Bloomburg
Atlanta
Princeton
Farmersville
Greenville
Campbell
Ridgeway
Weaver
Saltillo
Sulphur Springs
Como
Pickton
Brashear
HUNT
Lavon Lake
Allen
Copeville
Caddo Mills
Lavon
Plano
Wylie
Lewisville
Grapevine Lake
Carrollton
Richardson
Royse City
Cash
Quinlan
Farmers Branch
DALLAS
Garland
Rockwall
ROCKWALL
Lake Ray Hubbard
Lake Tawakoni
Euless
Irving
Dallas
Grand Prairie
Arlington
Forney
Mesquite
Balch Springs
Seagoville
Kleberg
Hutchins
Duncanville
Cedar Hill
Lancaster
Terrell
Elmo
Wills Point
Crandall
Kaufman
Scurry
Rosser
KAUFMAN
Kemp
Tolosa
Mabank
Phalba
Canton
VAN ZANDT
Myrtle Springs
Edgewood
Fruitvale
Grand Saline
Sabine River
RAINS
Emory
Lone Oak Point
Yantis
WOOD
Winnsboro
Lake Quitman
Lake Winnsboro
Quitman
Alba
Lake Holbrook
Mineola
Lake Hawkins
Crow
Van
Garden Valley
Ben Wheeler
Lindale
Mount Sylvan
Hawkins
Big Sandy
Gladewater
Winona
Lake Cypress Springs
Lake Monticello
Mount Pleasant
Pittsburg
Leesburg
Newsome
CAMP
Cason
Ellison Creek Res.
Lone Star
Daingerfield
Hughes Spring
Linden
Bivins
Rodessa
McLeod
CASS
Avinger
MARION
Vivian
Smithland
Jefferson
Lake O' the Pines
Ore City
Bettie
UPSHUR
Gilmer
Pritchett
Glenwood
Lake Gladewater
West Mountain
Diana
GREGG
Harleton
Caddo Lake
Mooringsport
Woodlawn
Karnack
HARRISON
Marshall
Hallsville
Jonesville
Longview
Waskom
Kilgore
Lakeport
Lake Cherokee
Tatum
Panola
De Berry
Midlothian
Venus
Red Oak
Ferris
Palmer
ELLIS
Waxahachie
Ennis
Alma
Rice
Seven Points
Tool
Eustace
Cedar Creek Reservoir
Murchison
Brownsboro
Chandler
Tyler
SMITH
Overton
Bardwell
Forreston
Bardwell Lake
Avalon
Italy
Blooming Grove
Milford
Frost
Mertens
Brandon
Bynum
Malone
Barry
Corsicana
Powell
Kerens
Trinidad
Malakoff
Athens
HENDERSON
Navarro Mills Lake
Richland
NAVARRO
Eureka
Cayuga
Montalba
Lake Athens
Coffee City
Larue
Poynor
Frankston
Lake Palestine
Cuney
Reese
Jacksonville
Lake Jacksonville
Whitehouse
Lake Tyler
Bullard
Troup
Mount Selman
New Summerfield
Arp
Pontal
Lake Striker
New London
Turnertown
Price
RUSK
Chapman
Martin Creek Lake
Henderson
Beckville
PANOLA
Carthage
Clayton
Murval Reservoir
Tenaha
Timpson
Mount Enterprise
Concord
Caledonia
Joaquin
Paxton
Logansport
SHELBY

Dallas and Northeast Texas

Dallas, Rockwall, Rains, Wood, Camp, Cass, Marion, Harrison, Upshur, Gregg, Van Zandt and Kaufman Counties

This part of Texas is served by more freeways than any other area in the state. No other city in Texas has more than two interstate freeways. Dallas has four. I-45 connects Dallas with Houston and Galveston. Interstate 35 extends southward to Austin and San Antonio and the border and northward to Oklahoma. Interstate 30 links Dallas with Texarkana to the east. Interstate 20 extends from Dallas to the border in both directions. The area included in this section of this book is roughly the territory between Interstate 30 and Interstate 20 East including the city and county of Dallas.

We are not advocating that this area be viewed from the interstates or judged by what can be seen from the interstates. Texas has some of the finest interstate freeways you can find anywhere. But interstate freeways are much the same wherever you find them. The billboards, the trucks, the chain restaurants and the chain motels are about the same on the freeways in Texas as they are on the freeways in any other state. Much of Texas is served by freeways, but there is not much of Texas on the freeways.

The real Texas is on the roads and highways the interstate travelers never see. And traveling the backroads in Texas is no hardship. The network of secondary roads in this state is second to none. The area covered in this section includes U.S. Highway 80. U.S. 80 was the primary highway from the Louisiana border to El Paso before the interstate system was built. Interstate 20 follows the same route as U.S. 80 west of

1

1) The new Reunion Tower and Hyatt Hotel in downtown Dallas help give the central business district an ultra modern look. In naming his tower, Oilman Ray Hunt used the name of a French commune that tried to establish itself near Dallas in the 1850s.

Dallas. But Interstate 20 runs south of U.S. 80 for most of the distance between Dallas and the Louisiana Line. Old U.S. 80 is still here. Driving U.S. 80 anywhere between Terrell and Marshall is like driving in another time. The billboards and the trucks have all gone to the interstate. U.S. 80 is wide and smooth and relatively free of traffic, and it goes through towns instead of around them. Try U.S. 80.

DALLAS COUNTY

The easternmost city of Texas is Bon Wier in Jasper County. But the most eastern city is and always has been Dallas. This may be partly the result of a conscious effort on the part of the residents. But it probably results mostly from the fact that Dallas has always been a center for commercial interests

2) The old Dallas County Courthouse downtown is no longer used by county personnel. It was vacated in early 1978 and engineers began studying ways to preserve it. The exterior is red sandstone. 2

with close ties to eastern cities. Dallas is an important banking and insurance and merchandising center. It is the home of the State Fair of Texas. The state did not decide to have a fair in Dallas. Dallas decided to have a fair and call it the State Fair. It is the Dallas way.

The first settler here was John Neely Bryan. He built a log cabin in 1841. It is still preserved in the Dallas County Historical Plaza in downtown Dallas.

Bryan donated the block of land for the Dallas County courthouse square. The county was organized in 1846 and named in honor of U.S. Vice President George Mifflin Dallas. The Dallas County Courthouse was built in 1890.

John Neely Bryan was the original Dallas promoter and he set the pattern for later boosters. Bryan spread such glowing reports about his settlement on the Trinity in the early 1840's that settlers sometimes came in expecting to find a city. One of the settlers arriving with the Peters' Colonists in 1844 wrote in his journal that the town of Dallas he had heard so much about turned out to have two log cabins and about 10 or 12 people. But Dallas eventually became everything Bryan hoped for, and it has fulfilled every promise its promoters have made ever since.

Bryan remained a prominent figure in Dallas business and civic affairs for many years, and he was on hand as a member of the official welcoming delegation when the first train reached Dallas on the new Houston and Texas Central Rail-

1

1) John Neely Bryan was the intrepid settler who built the first log cabin in Dallas in 1841 and it 2) is preserved in the Dallas County Historical Plaza in downtown Dallas. Bryan was the first Dallas booster and his enthusiastic promotion of the settlement brought an influx of colonists that caused a town to develop and grow. It has been growing ever since.

2

road in July of 1872. The Texas and Pacific reached Dallas in 1873. The population jumped from 1,200 to 7,000, and Dallas was on its way.

The railroads and the early hotels built to accommodate the rail travelers made Dallas an early center for commercial travelers. The commercial travelers were known then as drummers, and one of the early drummers' hotels is preserved today in the Old City Park at 1400 South Ervay Street. The Dallas County Heritage Society maintains the park as a museum. There are several other buildings from the 19th Century, including the Millermore Mansion from 1862, a log schoolhouse from 1847, and a railroad depot from 1875. The

3

4

3) This is the way some of Dallas' earliest stores looked in the 19th Century. 4) The drummers' hotel is where traveling salesmen stayed when they came through Dallas in the city's early days. These and other historic buildings make up the old City Park preserved by the Dallas Heritage Society.

buildings in Old City Park are open from 10:00 a.m. to 4:00 p.m. Tuesdays, Wednesdays, Thursdays and Fridays and from 1:30 to 4:30 p.m. on weekends. There is an admission charge for touring the buildings but none for the park.

A Frenchman named Victor Prosper Considerant made a tour of East Texas in 1852 and 1853 and convinced himself that it was an ideal place for an experimental socialist colony he wanted to establish. Considerant went home to France and organized a colony and sent it over. The colonists bought a tract of land on the West Fork of the Trinity near the settle-

1

1) Among the Old City Park structures is this early Texas home built by Howard Hughes' grandfather. 2) Mansions that measured both the success and stature of a family began to group themselves in the Dallas area known as Swiss Avenue. Some of the Swiss Avenue homes today are among the best-preserved in the state and some are listed in the National Register of Historic Places.

2

ment of Dallas. They named their colony La Reunion, and they started farming. They did not know very much about farming, and their colony failed. La Reunion was dissolved after a few years. Some of the colonists returned to France. Some moved to New Orleans, and some remained in Dallas. The name of their commune has been borrowed by oilman Ray Hunt for his spectacular Reunion Tower in downtown Dallas.

Swiss and German settlers arrived here in the 1870's. The Swiss settled along the street that is still known as Swiss Avenue. The Germans settled along what they called Germania Street. Americans tried to disown some of their German heritage during World War I. Many German names were changed. Germania Street became Liberty Street. Part of Swiss Avenue is now listed in the National Register of Historic Places because of the number of elegant old homes

3

4

3) The Texas State Fair cuts loose each October in Dallas. It is a major spectacle. Texans of all ages from all over the state flock here for livestock competition, exhibits of all kinds and fun on the midway. 4) This is how the state fair looked in 1903.

still standing here. The A. H. Belo home at 2115 Ross, and the Dallas Union Station at 400 South Houston are also listed in the National Register.

The State Fair of Texas is held at the Fairgrounds in Dallas every year in October. The University of Texas plays Oklahoma in the Cotton Bowl then, and the Cotton Bowl game itself is played here every New Year's Day. There is something going on at the Fairgrounds most of the rest of the year, too. There are 33 permanent rides on the Midway operating the year around.

The Dallas Museum of Fine Arts in the Park is open every

1 *1) Railroad buffs can see pretty much what a rail arrival in Dallas looked like long ago by visiting the Age of Steam Museum. It is on the Texas State Fairgrounds and open Sundays most of the year.*

day except Monday and there is no charge for admission. The Dallas Museum of Natural History here is open every day and free.

The Texas Hall of State with books and documents covering 400 years of history is open every day. The Age of Steam Museum on the northwest corner of the Fairground is open during the Fair and on Sundays only the rest of the year. This is an old railroad station and a collection of other railroad relics.

The first Fair was held in Dallas in 1859. There was another one in 1862. The Fair began to be held on a more or less regular basis in 1872. The Texas Centennial Exposition was staged here in 1936.

The *Dallas Morning News* calls itself the oldest business institution in Texas. The *Dallas Morning News* is descended from the *Dallas Herald* and the *Galveston Daily News.* The *Herald* was founded in Dallas by James W. Latimer and John W. Swindells. It became the *Dallas Weekly Herald* in 1873 and then became the *Dallas Daily Herald* in 1874. The paper was absorbed in 1885 into the *Dallas Morning News* established the same year by A. H. Belo and Company as a branch of the *Galveston Daily News.* There was no connection between the old *Dallas Herald* and the *Dallas Times Herald,*

2) Dealey Plaza is named for one of Dallas' most noted publishers. It was here, November 22, 1963, that President Kennedy was assasinated. The city erected this memorial and there is a Kennedy Museum nearby. 2

born in 1888 from the merger of the *Dallas Evening Times* and the *Dallas Evening Herald.*

Augustus Horatio Belo went to work for the *Galveston News* in 1865. He became the principal owner of the paper when its publisher, Willard Richardson, died in 1875. George Bannerman Dealcy went to work as an office boy in the offices of the *Galveston Daily News* in 1870 and moved up fast. Belo sent Dealey to Dallas as manager of the *Dallas Morning News* in 1885. The Dealey family bought out the Belos in 1926 and later sold the *Galveston Daily News* to the Moodys. Dealey continued to run the *Dallas Morning News* until he died in 1944. He was recognized then as the dean of American journalists, and it was for him that Dealey Plaza was named.

But Dealey Plaza is unfortunately better known for the tragedy that occurred here November 22, 1963. President John F. Kennedy was shot to death that day as he and Mrs. Kennedy and Governor and Mrs. John Connally were being driven through the plaza in an open Lincoln. The city has erected a memorial nearby at Main and Record. There is a Kennedy Museum at 501 Elm Street on the plaza.

The Texas School Book Depository Building where the presumed assassin waited for the Kennedy motorcade that day

1 *1) One of the landmarks of merchandising success in Dallas is the Neiman-Marcus store downtown. Neiman's has stores now in fashionable resorts and suburbs in other parts of the country. The original store has been doing business in this building near the original site downtown since 1914. The company was founded in 1907.*

has been acquired by Dallas County. There will be county offices in the building. There has been a little talk about making the top floor a memorial and museum, but there is strong sentiment against it.

The Texas Stadium where the Dallas Cowboys play their home games is in Irving. There are conducted tours of the playing field, the press box, the private suites and the dressing rooms from 10:00 a.m. to 2:00 p.m. on weekdays, and at 11:00 a.m., 12:30 p.m. and 2:00 p.m. on Saturdays and holidays. (There are no tours, though, on game days.) The stadium is on Loop 12 at Carpenter Freeway in Irving.

Love Field is one of the oldest airports in the state. It was established in 1914 as an Army air training base. The first airmail flight and the first passenger flight in Texas originated here. And it was here in 1963 that Lyndon Johnson took the oath of office as President after President Kennedy was murdered. Love Field still handles some commercial air traffic, but most flights now arrive and depart from the big Dallas-Fort Worth Airport. The DFW Airport is partly in Tarrant County. The Six Flags Park and the Dallas Rangers' baseball stadium are entirely in Tarrant County. The airport is on State Highway 183 at Grapevine. Six Flags and the Rangers' stadium are on Interstate 30 at Arlington.

2 *2) The Dallas County Trade Mart draws buyers and exhibitors from all over the nation to attend apparel and furniture exhibitions. 3) Robert Cooke Buckner was an early Texas pioneer and Baptist pastor. Starting with this cabin, he gave shelter to a few orphan children and ultimately established the large Buckner Orphans Home.* 3

One of the few Texas buildings designed by the late Frank Lloyd Wright is the Dallas Theater Center at 3636 Turtle Creek Boulevard. Plays and musicals are presented here the year around.

Southern Methodist University has grown into one of the major educational institutions in the country since it began classes with 706 students in 1915. The SMU campus is in the suburb of University Park at Hillcrest and Mockingbird.

Dallas is one of the principal fashion centers in the world. Buyers come from everywhere for the apparel marts and furniture marts and other shows held at the World Trade Center at 2300 Stemmons Freeway. A few areas of the Center, including a restaurant or two, are open to the public, but most of the events at the Dallas World Trade Center are closed to everybody except the exhibitors and buyers.

There are elevated observation points accessible to the public in Dallas at The Southland Center, and at the First National Bank, and at the new Reunion Tower. The Southland Center has a restaurant and lounge on the 41st floor open from 10:00 a.m. to 8:00 p.m. daily. The First National Bank at Elm and Akard has an observation deck on the 50th floor. It is open 9:00 a.m. to 5:00 p.m. weekdays, and there is a 25¢ charge. The Reunion Tower has an observation platform and a restaurant above it. The tower is 561 feet tall. It is at Liveoak and Pearl. There is an admission fee.

1 *1) This unusual underground rock formation in Rockwall County gave rise to the theory that some ancient settlers may have built it. This stone outcropping gave the city and county their name.*

These are some of the Dallas County sites with historical markers:

The site of La Reunion Colony, Steven Park in Oak Cliff, on Hampton just off Colorado. Clyde Barrow is buried in a little cemetery on Fort Worth Avenue, nearby. Vandals have stolen his headstone several times.

The Alexander home at 4607 Ross Avenue; The Ambassador Hotel, 1312 Ervay; R. C. Buckner Log Cabin, Buckner Orphans' Home, Samuel and Buckner.

ROCKWALL COUNTY

Rockwall County is one of the smaller counties in the state. It covers only 147 square miles. Rockwall County was organized in 1873. The county seat is the city of Rockwall. The present courthouse here was built in 1939. The area is now part of the Dallas metropolitan area. There is some industry, but many of the residents are commuting to jobs in Dallas.

Anglo settlement in this county began about 1846. In 1852, a man named Terry Wade made the discovery that gave the city and county their name. Wade found a strange rock formation under the ground. He dug out some of the dirt and found that the formation very much resembled a rock wall that might have been made by man. It is pretty well settled now that the formation is a natural one, but there were some theories earlier that it might have been a relic from some ancient civilization. Such a wall would not have been beyond

2

2) The courthouse at Rockwall handles the business for Texas' smallest county — 147 square miles in size. 3) The Rains County Courthouse at Emory. Here is another of those cases in Texas where the early residents thought so highly of a local citizen — in this case Emory Rains — that they used his first and last names in naming their city and county.

3

the engineering abilities of the Incas. But evidently nobody as smart as the Incas lived in this part of the world until we came.

Lake Ray Hubbard on the west fork of the Trinity River gives Rockwall County many miles of waterfront. The lake is part of the Dallas Municipal Water Supply System and there are some excellent resorts around its shores. The lake covers nearly 23,000 acres.

RAINS COUNTY

Rains is another county where the city and the county both are named for the same man. The man was Emory Rains. He was one of the earliest settlers in East Texas. Rains came to the Red River Country from Tennessee in 1826. He served in the Senate in the days of the Republic, and he served in the State House of Representatives after Texas became a state.

1

1) Emory Rains came to Texas before the 1836 revolution and was active in politics from the time the Republic of Texas came into being. He served as a senator in the second and third congresses of the Republic. He served in the legislature when Texas became a state. He helped survey the county that bears his name. 2) An early photo of Emory looks like a western movie set.

2

Rains was 70 years old when this county was organized and named in his honor. The residents held an election to pick a county seat and a name for it. They chose a town that had been called Springville and decided to change the name of it to Emory. Emory has been the county seat of the county named for Emory Rains ever since.

Emory is one of our smaller county seats, but it certainly is not the smallest. There are about 1,000 people in Emory, but that is about 20 times the population of Mentone, the county seat of Loving County in far west Texas.

The present courthouse at Emory was built in 1908. It is the third courthouse the county has had. The first one burned in 1879, and the fire destroyed all the county's records.

Rains County is in the valley of the Sabine River and part of the east shore of Lake Tawakoni lies within the county's

3

3) Some of the earliest settlers in Rains County are buried here in the Hooker Cemetery on FM 513, northeast of Tawakoni.

borders. There is a lot of submerged timber in the lake, and the fishing is reputed to be good. Tawakoni is an Indian name.

The Tawakoni Indians were part of the Wichita tribe. They were not natives of Texas, but some of them lived in the state for a time in the 1700's and 1800's. One of the earliest settlers in what is now Rains County was J. H. Hooker. He established a mill on the Sabine here in the late 1840's. Farmers brought grain to Hooker's Mill from as far away as Dallas.

WOOD COUNTY

Wood County was organized in 1850. The county was named for George T. Wood. He was a political and military leader in East Texas in the 1840's and 1850's, and the second Governor of Texas.

Wood came to Texas from Georgia in 1839 with his family and three dozen slaves. He built a plantation on the banks of the Trinity in what is now San Jacinto County. Wood served a term in the Congress of the Republic. He was elected a State Senator after Texas joined the union. He won a reputation as a military hero during the war with Mexico, and he was elected Governor in 1847.

This county and the county seat of Tyler County both are named for Wood. Wood introduced the bill that created Tyler County while he was serving as a Senator and the people of the county showed their appreciation by naming their county seat Woodville. Wood apparently never lived in Wood County or Woodville, either. He and his wife both are buried in

1

2 *1) The management of Wood County is done from this 1920s courthouse in Quitman. 2) This mid-19th Century home was built by Colonel James A. Stinson near Quitman. Future Governor James S. Hogg married Sallie Stinson in this house.*

San Jacinto County where their plantation was. The site is near the present town of Pointblank.

The county seat of Wood County is the city of Quitman. The present courthouse was built in 1925. The town is named for John A. Quitman. He never lived in Texas, but Texans felt grateful to him because he organized and financed a company of volunteers for the revolution in 1836, and because he later helped organize opinion in the United States in favor of the annexation of Texas. Quitman lived most of his life in Mississippi.

Quitman was for a time the home of James Stephen Hogg. Hogg was the first native Texan to be elected Governor of the

3

3) This museum is south of Quitman in the Governor Hogg Shrine State Park and 4) this is the birthplace of Ima Hogg at Mineola. The late Miss Ima became one of the state's leading and most beloved philanthropists.

4

state. He was born near Rusk in what is now Cherokee County. He went into newspaper work there and then worked on a paper in Tyler. He had his own newspaper in Longview before he moved to Quitman to run his own paper. Hogg was studying law while he was working on his newspapers and eventually was elected Justice of the Peace and then County Attorney and then District Attorney. Hogg was elected Attorney General of Texas in 1886 and he was elected Governor in 1890. Hogg served as Governor until 1895 and then retired to practice law. He made investments in city real estate and oil lands that eventually made him rich.

Hogg married Sallie Stinson of Quitman during the time he was studying law. They were married at the fancy home Sallie's parents maintained a few miles outside Quitman. Sallie's father was Colonel James A. Stinson. It was fortunate he had a big house. There was a storm the night of the wed-

1

1) The Collins-Haines House at Quitman is a fine example of an early Texas brick home, built on classical lines. 2) The Wilson House at Mineola was built during the great days of the railroad passenger trains. It was then the Bailey Hotel. New owners have restored the dining room and furnished it with antiques. They serve meals. They plan to restore the rooms too and open the hotel again to the public.

2

ding, and all of the wedding guests had to spend the night at the Stinson home.

The Stinson home has been moved, and it is preserved now in the Governor Hogg Shrine State Park on State Highway 37 at the southern edge of Quitman. This little park is the former property of the Wood County Old Settlers' Reunion Association and the old settlers still hold their reunions here. Also in the park are the little house where Jim Hogg and his wife lived after they were first married and the Miss Ima Hogg Museum, named for Governor Hogg's only daughter. The park is open to the public every day. The buildings are open every day except Tuesday and Wednesday.

There are two towns in Wood County larger than Quitman. They are Mineola and Winnsboro. Mineola is in the southwestern corner of the county on U.S. 80. The name sounds Indian, but it is not. This town grew up around a railroad sta-

3) Marcus Dewitt Carlock, Sr. built this colonial mansion at Winnsboro in 1903. And he built it to last. It has 17 rooms, four porches, double floors, five ply walls — and enough brick in the foundation to build a five-room brick house. 3

tion that railroad man Ira Evans named in honor of his daughter, Ola, and the daughter's friend, Minnie Patton. Governor Hogg's daughter Ima was born here in 1882.

Winnsboro is on the northern edge of the county on State Highway 37. It was named for early settler John Wynn. The Handbook of Texas says the name began to be spelled with an "I" instead of a "Y" because the local newspaper was short of "Y's" and had plenty of "I's". Winnsboro was a small settlement when the railroad came through in 1876 and turned it into a town. By 1882, Winnsboro had a population of more than 1,000. There was an opera house, and there were several mills, gins and a factory making carriages and wagons.

Several of the homes and buildings put up during the town's heyday are still standing here. One of the most imposing is the home Marcus Dewitt Carlock built in 1903 at 407 South Main Street.

Winnsboro is headquarters for the Autumn Trails celebration in October, when the trees turn red.

It is an interesting coincidence that two residents of this county owned the same plantation in another county at different times without ever knowing each other. Martin Varner was one of the early settlers of Texas. He was one of Stephen F. Austin's original 300 colonists. He built the Varner plantation in Brazoria County that later became the home of Governor Jim Hogg. Varner moved to the Wood County area in 1844 after he sold the plantation in Brazoria County. Hogg

1

1) Colonel John Lafayette Camp led the 14th Texas Infantry for the Confederacy in the Civil War. He was captured twice and wounded twice. So, he may not have been too surprised when the U.S. Congress refused to seat him as a Texas Congressman right after the Civil War. He was later a noted Texas jurist and Camp County is named in his honor. 2) The Camp County Courthouse at Pittsburg recently observed its 50th birthday.

2

did not buy the plantation until years later. Varner was killed in a dispute over a debt before Jim Hogg was born. The plantation they both owned in Brazoria County is now a park, donated to the state by Hogg's daughter, Ima.

CAMP COUNTY

Camp County was created in 1874 and named in honor of Confederate Colonel John Lafayette Camp. Colonel Camp had moved from Tennessee to Texas in 1849. The colonel was elected to the U.S. House of Representatives in the election immediately following the war. But the Congress of the United States was not having any truck with Confederate colonels at that point, so Camp never was seated. He did serve later as a member of the Texas Senate and he was also a District Judge.

3

3) It is not listed in the Michelin Guide but the Pittsburg Hot Links Cafe in Camp County draws attention and diners from miles around. One school of culinary thought in Texas contends that good hot link sausage is almost an art form. It is a Pittsburgh specialty. 4) This is a Camp County reminder of another type of industry in another age. One of the early flying machines was built here.

4

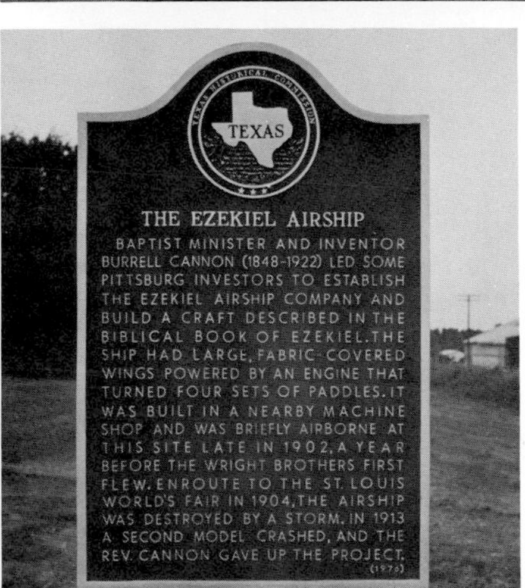

5) The Wright Brothers were still making bicycles when a Texas inventor named Burrell Cannon was building his airship. This marker at Pittsburg in Camp County attests to his partial success in flying the thing here in 1902. Cannon's experiments were financed by a stock company that raised $20,000 in 1901. Cannon gave up his dream of flying machines after his first two planes were destroyed in mishaps.

5

1 *1) John Sheppard built this home for his family in 1884 at Pittsburg while he was a judge. The house has eight fireplaces and a secret passageway between the floors. Sheppard was later elected to Congress.*

The county seat of Camp County is the city of Pittsburg. It was not named for the city in Pennsylvania. This Pittsburg was founded and named by W. H. Pitts. He came here from Georgia and settled in 1854. The present courthouse at Pittsburg was built in 1928.

There is some ranching and some farming here. The county has some oil and a lot of timber.

Camp County has the oldest Carnegie Library in Texas. It is at 200 Rusk Street in Pittsburg.

A marker at 217 Mount Pleasant in Pittsburg testifies that John L. Sheppard lived here. Sheppard was a member of the U.S. House of Representatives and the father of U.S. Senator Morris Sheppard.

CASS COUNTY

Cass County was organized in 1846. It was named in honor of United States Senator Lewis Cass. The Senator was not a Texan. He represented Michigan in the Senate, but he was one of the leaders in the move to get Texas annexed to the Union. Lewis Cass was a Yankee, and so Texans came to consider his name an embarrassment during the Civil War. The name of this county was changed from Cass to Davis in 1861 to honor Confederate President Jefferson Davis. It was changed back to Cass in 1871.

Cass County originally included the area that later became

2

3

2) The town of Linden was only about seven years old in 1859 when the Cass County government began building this courthouse. But the Civil War came along and the building was not completed until after the war was over. 3) The Matthews-Powell House at Queen City is one of the well-preserved historic homes in Cass County. It is located on Miller Street.

1 *1) One of Atlanta's historic landmarks is the Smith-Hoyt-Youngs House at Hiram and Harvey Streets. It was built in 1887 by J. P. McReynolds. This house had the first indoor bath and first telephone in Atlanta. 2) This Cass County dwelling at Horace Springs is typical of the shelters the early settlers built with their own timber.* 2

Marion County. The original county seat was the city of Jefferson. But Jefferson went with Marion County when the division occurred in 1860. The town of Linden then became the county seat of what remained of Cass County. Linden was founded in 1852 and named for a town in Tennessee. The present courthouse was started in 1859 and completed after the Civil War.

Farming and lumbering were the principal activities here in the beginning. Iron foundries were established at Hughes Springs in 1856 and at Queen City in 1877 when iron ore was found in the area. The oil was discovered in 1935. The minerals produce more income now than the farming.

The principal city in Cass County is Atlanta. It has benefited more from the oil business than Linden has.

The Atlanta State Park is northwest of Atlanta on Farm Road 1154. The park is on the south shore of Lake Wright Patman. This is one of the Class I Parks. There are provisions for camping, picnicking, swimming, fishing and skiing. The park covers more than 1,400 acres. There is an admission charge of $1.00 per vehicle in all the Class I Parks in the state unless you have an annual permit or a parklands passport.

Hughes Springs on State Highway 11 at the eastern edge of Cass County is one of the older settlements in the area. It was established in 1839 by a man named Reece Hughes. He built an iron foundry here and had it taken away from him during the Civil War. Hughes was not in sympathy with secession. The Confederates needed his foundry so they just seized it and operated for the benefit of the Confederacy for the duration. Hughes Springs enjoyed a brief boom as a health resort after the railroad arrived in 1876.

3) One of the magnificent annual sights along Texas highways is the springtime blanket of blue, yellow, white and red wildflowers. Many of the flowers are planted by personnel of the Texas Highway Department. The department would rather you not pick them. 3

Hughes Springs, Linden and Avinger collaborate to stage the Texas Wildflower Trails Festival each spring. It is usually in late April. You can see most of the wildflowers native to Texas during this period by driving State Highway 11 from Linden to Hughes Springs, State Highway 49 from Hughes Springs to Avinger and State Highway 155 from Avinger back to Linden. There are musical programs and other special events during the festival.

Many of the wildflowers growing along the sides of the roads and highways in Texas were planted there by the men of the Texas Department of Highways and Public Transportation. They gather up seeds at the end of the blooming season each year and scatter them along the medians and roadsides. They do not encourage the picking of wildflowers on the rights-of-way. But nobody has been arrested for it, yet.

MARION COUNTY

Marion County was separated from Cass County and established as a county in 1860. It was named for General Francis Marion. He was one of the heroes of the American Revolution. Jefferson had been the county seat of Cass County and before that it was the county seat of the still larger Jefferson County. So Jefferson was a substantial town when Marion County was established. It was founded in 1836 and named for President Thomas Jefferson. The present courthouse was built in 1934.

1

1) The Marion County Courthouse at Jefferson is a relatively new structure by Jefferson's standards. This was one of the earliest river ports in Texas and most early settlers thought the town would grow to be a major city someday. 2) "The Magnolias" is one of the elegant old homes left from the days when Jefferson was at the height of its prosperity. Note the full length windows and fluted columns.

2.

This was one of the busiest and richest and most important towns in the state in the late 1860's and early 1870's. The waterways were still the principal traffic arteries then, and Jefferson was a major port. The town sits on Big Cypress Bayou at the eastern end of Caddo Lake. Big Cypress Bayou was one of those waterways in the Red River watershed that was swollen by the rafts and logjams that clogged the Red River for so long. People were not conscious at the time that it was an unnatural situation, and they had no idea that the water level would drop drastically when the Army Engineers finished clearing the debris from the main channel of the Red River in 1874. What they did know was that they had deep water at their docks at the foot of Polk Street. River steamers

3

4

3) You would have been able to catch a river steamer heading for New Orleans if you had come to this spot in the 1870s. It was widely believed then that clearing debris from the Red River channel would enhance Jefferson's position as a port city. It did not happen. The water level dropped and today only small boats operate here. 4) Railroad tycoon Jay Gould might not be entirely happy to know that his personal railway car has become a tourist attraction in Jefferson — the town that snubbed him and his railroad.

could travel from here to the Red River to the Mississippi River and down to New Orleans. They made the most of it. Jefferson rivaled Galveston, exporting the products of Texas farms and plantations and importing manufactured goods from all over the world. The people of Jefferson lived well, and the evidence of their comfortable life is visible all over Jefferson today.

Jefferson was so satisfied with what it was that it failed to accommodate itself to the changes the spread of the railroads brought to the state. Riverports that had better luck with their water level than Jefferson did were wiped out when they failed to get rail service. Jefferson elected not to get rail service. Railroad tycoon Jay Gould wanted to bring a rail line to the city. But he wanted something in return. It was a time when governmental agencies were offering all kinds of inducements to railroad builders. The State of Texas was giving the Texas and Pacific Railroad Company big blocks of

1) The Excelsior House started in the 1850s. It is still renting rooms in Jefferson. Many of the most famous Texans and Texas visitors of the 19th Century came here by riverboat — and stayed at the Excelsior House.

land for every mile of track it built on its line across the state. Jay Gould could be forgiven for expecting that Jefferson would offer him money or land or both. Jefferson refused. The railroad went to Marshall instead and Marshall has been prospering ever since. Gould predicted that the decision against his railroad would spell the end of Jefferson. Jefferson is no longer a major commercial center. But it still has the air and atmosphere of a prosperous river port of the 19th century, minus the riverboats. And you can still navigate the waters of Big Cypress Bayou if you bring your own boat. There is a public launching ramp alongside the bridge where the U.S. 59 Business Route crosses the bayou at the foot of Polk Street, about where the old steamboat landing was.

There is evidence that the people here still think they made the right answer to Jay Gould. Jefferson has acquired the palatial private railroad car Gould used on his travels around his railroad empire in the 80's. The car is parked on a lot across the street from the old Excelsior House Hotel on Austin Street. Visitors can tour it for 50¢ each.

The Excelsior House is one of the oldest hotels in the state. The oldest part of it goes back to the 1850's. The hotel is still in operation. It has 14 rooms for rent, and each one has its own bath. The plumbing was added around the turn of the century. There is no dining room. But the Club Cafe around the corner has good, plain Texas food.

2

2) Among the innovations spawned in Jefferson was a brand new idea in 1875: making ice artificially. This historical marker is on the site of the early plant. 3) Dramatic presentations are still staged during the month of May when Jefferson holds its annual historical pilgrimage. Some of the old homes are opened to visitors then.

3

Jefferson had one of the first breweries in Texas. The first artificial ice plant in the world was here, and Jefferson was the first city in Texas to use artificial gas for lighting. The gas plant was at Lafayette and Market. The ice plant was on State Highway 49 where the Blackburn Syrup works are now.

There is an authentic old apothecary shop and general store at 312 East Broadway. The old Red River Warehouse Company is on Dallas Street. The old Rosebud Saloon is at 109 Vale Street. The Jefferson Playhouse is on Henderson Street. A play depicting a sensational murder that actually occurred during the town's heyday is presented here during the annual Jefferson Historical Pilgrimage the first weekend in May. Some of the old homes are open during the Pilgrimage, too.

1

2

Jefferson has dozens of 19th Century homes in good and comfortable condition including 1) the "House of the Seasons" and 2) "The Manse," built in 1839.

There are picturesque and historic homes all over Jefferson. More than 30 of the homes and buildings here have historical medallions. One of the oldest is The Manse built in 1839 at Delta and Alley Streets. One of the most imposing is the House of the Seasons at the same intersection.

The Jefferson Historical Society Museum is in an old Federal Courthouse building at 223 W. Austin, almost next door

3) This former Harrison County Courthouse has now become a repository of important artifacts and historical objects from the county's past. It is in downtown Marshall. 3

to the Excelsior House Hotel. The building was built in 1888. It has a basement and two and a half floors above the ground, and there are many interesting exhibits. They include an art collection, old furniture and costumes, a collection of antique toys and a big assortment of kitchen and farm implements.

Many of the early settlers of the west passed this way, and many of those settlers got their plows from the Kelly Plow Company of Kellyville. Kellyville was just east of Jefferson and the Kelly Plow Company operated here until a fire destroyed the factory in 1882. The Kelly Company moved then to Longview and later closed. The company's records are now in the library of the Stephen F. Austin University in Nacogdoches. Some of the plows and other items from the factory are on exhibit in the basement of the Jefferson Historical Society Museum. The museum is open daily. There is a fee of $1.00 for adults and 50¢ for children.

HARRISON COUNTY

Harrison County was organized in 1839. It was named for Jonas Harrison. He came here from New York in 1820. Harrison was an alcalde in what is now Shelby County while Texas was still Mexican territory. He was one of the early advocates of Independence. He was a lawyer and he handled the legal details of Sam Houston's divorce from his first wife.

1

1) Experts say this is the oldest pottery yet found west of the Mississippi. It was unearthed in Harrison County and is credited to the early Caddo Indians. This is part of the pottery display in the Harrison County Museum in the old courthouse. 2) Clay around Marshall is ideally suited to pottery use and workmen may be seen practicing their craft at the Marshall Pottery Factory southeast of the city.

2

The county seat is Marshall. Marshall benefited from Jefferson's decision not to be a railroad town in the 1870's. But Marshall was well on its way before that happened. This was plantation country before the Civil War. Marshall was a prosperous trading and manufacturing center. Factories here produced supplies for the Confederate forces throughout the war. Marshall was headquarters for Confederate Civil Authorities in the West after Vicksburg fell.

The present courthouse was built in 1966. It is one of the newer courthouses in the state, and it is the ninth courthouse Harrison County has had. Building courthouses is almost a

3

3) Nearly everything has some use to David Romero of Hallsville. He proves it with the garden he made of discarded materials. It is a popular local attraction at Christmas.

major industry here. The previous courthouse is now a museum operated by the Harrison County Historical Society. It features Caddo artifacts and historical displays. Some of the Caddo pottery items here date back to 400 B.C. This is believed to be the oldest pottery yet found west of the Mississippi. The old courthouse museum is on Peter Whetstone Square in downtown Marshall.

The clay here is especially suited to making pottery, and Marshall is still a major pottery center. The Marshall Pottery Factory has a huge store on Farm Road 31 just southeast of the city. Marshall Pottery was established in 1895, and it has been operated by the Ellis family since 1905. It is open from 9:00 a.m. to 6:00 p.m. Monday through Saturday. Some of the pots are made on the premises. The merchandise in the store is not limited to local pottery. The company ships its pots all over the country in its own trucks, and the trucks bring back merchandise from other places for sale in the pottery supermarket on Farm Road 31.

At Hallsville, west of Marshall on U.S. 80, David Romero has created an unusual garden from cast-off and discarded materials. Romero decorates the garden so attractively at Christmas time that hundreds of people drive here to see it. Romero's Garden is on South Chestnut in Hallsville.

The first settlers came to the town that is now Marshall in 1839. There were Methodist, Baptist and Presbyterian Churches established here by 1850. The town was an educational center from the beginning. The first school was Van

1

1) Frank's Museum in this antique house at Marshall contains an exhibit of old dolls from various periods of history. 2) The old Starr mansion at Travis and Groves in Marshall is in excellent condition partly because of the way it was built. James Frank Starr called it Maplecroft when he built it in 1870 and he used shipbuilders to do his construction work. They built it to last.

2

Zandt College. The college became Marshall University and eventually was merged with the Marshall Public School system. Bishop College was established here and later moved to Dallas. Wiley College was founded here in 1873 by a former slave named Meshack Roberts. Wiley is still teaching black students. The campus is on Wiley at University. East Texas Baptist College began operating here in 1912 as the College of Marshall. The name was changed in 1944. East Texas Baptist is on North Orange Street.

One of the sights to see in Marshall is the old Ginnochio Hotel. C. A. Ginnochio was an Italian immigrant. He saw the need for a good hotel near the busy Marshall railroad depot, and he built one so fancy that it is now listed in the National Register of Historic Places. Many famous people stayed here. Maurice Barrymore was once wounded in a shooting scrape here. Ginnochio's has been restored. The restaurant is operating. The hotel is not. This building was built in 1896. Listed with it in the National Register of Historic Places are several

3) You could have ridden the stagecoach from Marshall to Karnack along this road in the 1880s. The road appears to be in about the same condition now as it must have been then. Stagecoach rides are among the features of the Stagecoach Days Celebration held here in Marshall each May. 4) This log cabin on Perry Drive in Marshall is a relic from 1842. It was built at another location originally. The Hobard Key family moved it to this location in 1938.

old Victorian homes including the Ginnochio home at 615 N. Washington.

There is a doll museum with a large collection of old dolls at 211 W. Grand Avenue in Marshall. It is Franks Museum. There is an admission charge.

Harrison County has given Texas two governors. Edward Clark and Pendleton Murrah both were from Marshall.

These are some of the sites in Harrison County with historical markers:

402 South Bolivar Street, Marshall. Confederate sympathizers from Missouri had a kind of shadow government here during the Civil War. Missouri stayed with the Union. The southern sympathizers set up an office here and called it the Confederate Government of Missouri. The building is gone. There is a medical clinic at the site now.

1 *1) The late President Lyndon Johnson's wife, Lady Bird, was born in this house in Karnack. It was built before the Civil War. 2) Some of the most elegant homes of the mid-19th Century featured the kind of broad stairway seen on the Piece House in Marshall.* 2

407 West Travis, Marshall. This is a mansion James Frank Starr built in 1870 and called Maplecroft. He had shipbuilders build it and it is sturdy.

510 North Bolivar, Marshall. Here is one of the oldest brick homes in the county. It was built in 1846 for a freight hauling contractor named W. M. Patillo.

303 Perry Drive, Marshall. This log cabin was built sometime before 1842 at another location. It was moved to this location in 1938 by Mr. and Mrs. Hobard Key, Jr.

Highway 59, five miles north of Marshall. The Henderson House is built around a building that had been used as a stagecoach stop.

There is an old stagecoach road running northeastward out of Marshall toward Karnack. It is unpaved. It remains in much the same condition it must have been in during the 1880's and 1890's. You can ride a stagecoach here during Marshall's Stagecoach Days Celebration the third weekend in May every year. To find the old stagecoach road, take Poplar Street off U.S. 59 a few blocks north of U.S. 80. Poplar Street becomes Upper Port Caddo Road and Upper Port Caddo Road becomes Old Stagecoach Road. It eventually intersects State Highway 43.

Karnack near Caddo Lake is Mrs. Lyndon Johnson's home town. Mrs. Johnson was born Claudia Taylor. Her father was T. J. Taylor. He was a prosperous merchant. The house the Taylors were living in when Claudia was born had been built before the Civil War for a family named Andrews. It is made of bricks made by slaves.

Catfish fanciers will find several places around Caddo Lake specializing in catfish dinners. Pirate's Cove at Curley's Marina at Uncertain is one of them. Chief Cook Kizzie May

3

Some of East Texas' finest beauty spots are in the Caddo Lake area. 3) It is possible for the uninitiated boater to get lost in the many back channels and dark bayous. 4) Caddo Lake State Park at Karnack is situated on Big Cypress Bayou, just upstream from the lake proper. 5) The settlement of Uncertain on Caddo Lake got its name because steamboat captains in early days had trouble mooring their vessels.

4

5

1

1) A general store still going strong is the one run by Sam Vaughn at Jonesville. It is called the T. C. Lindsey General Store and Museum.

Hicks says this is her recipe for fixing catfish: Clean them, cut them up, wash them good, make sure they are left damp so the batter will stick. Prepare yellow cornmeal batter with salt and pepper mixed in just enough so you can taste the salt and pepper. Cook the fish in hot grease (about 360 degrees) in a deep fryer until golden brown (or until the fish float to the top).

The Caddo Lake State Park at Karnack is a Class I Park with provisions for camping, cabins for rent, boat ramps, playgrounds and fishing piers. The park is located about where old Port Caddo was located back in the days when there was more water in the lake and boats could travel between here and the Red River. There is the usual admission fee, and you can reserve spaces by writing to the Caddo Lake State Park, Route 2, Box 15, Karnack 75661, or by phoning 214-679-3351. The park is actually on Big Cypress Bayou a little upstream from the lake. The lake is one of the most picturesque in the state and uninitiated boatmen can easily get lost in the mysterious back channels and spooky bayous.

There is an old-time general store and museum at Jonesville, right up against the Louisiana line at the eastern edge of Harrison County. Sam Vaughn owns and operates the place. It is called the T. C. Lindsey General Store and Museum.

UPSHUR COUNTY

Upshur County was organized in 1846. It was named for

2

2) Somebody decided that this oil pump in Upshur County needed a little more visual appeal, so it was done up as a cowpony and rider. It is three miles west of Quitman on SH 154.

A. P. Upshur. He was United States Secretary of State under President John Tyler.

The earliest Anglo settler in what is now Upshur County was John Cotton. He came here in 1835. O. T. Boulware established the first trading post in the county at Cotton's Landing on Big Cow Bayou in 1838. Settlers from the old South brought in slaves and established cotton and tobacco plantations here in the years before the Civil War. The census of 1860 showed a population of 10,645 for the county. Slaves made up one third of the total.

Farming and ranching are the principal activities here, but there is substantial oil and gas production, too. The sweet potato has been a major factor here since 1890 and there is a Yamboree at Gilmer every year in October.

Gilmer is the county seat. It was established when the county was organized, and it was named for Thomas W. Gilmer. The present courthouse was built in 1936.

This was Caddo country. Remains of an ancient Indian culture have been found at Sand Hill. The excavation is nine miles northeast of Gilmer, about half a mile off a rural road. It is not easy to find. There are markers at the sites of other Indian villages in the Gilmer City Park and at the corner of Butler and Spring in Gilmer. Some of the Indians living here when the first white settlers came were Cherokees crowded out of their original homelands in the southeastern United States.

A lawyer named Oran Roberts ran a law school here in Gilmer between 1868 and 1874. It was not so much what he wanted to do, but what he was allowed to do. Roberts was an Associate Justice of the Texas Supreme Court in 1861. He

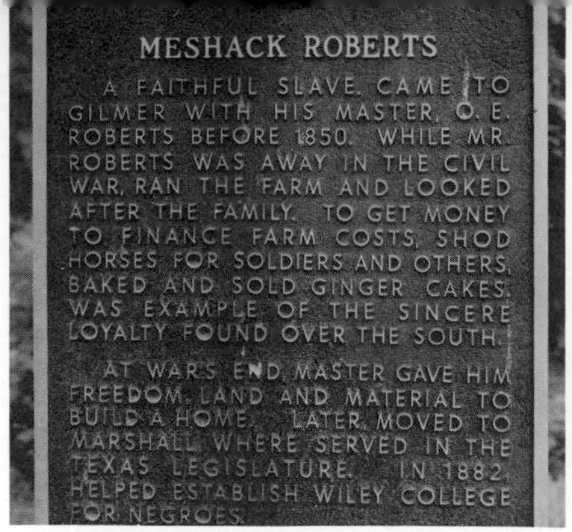

1) This historical marker just east of Gilmer pays tribute to a slave named Meshack Roberts. After the Civil War, Roberts served in the Texas Legislature and then helped to found Wiley College in Marshall.

helped engineer the state's secession from the Union and then became a colonel in the Confederate Army. He was a popular man. He was elected to the United States Senate at the end of the war. But the Senate refused to seat him because of his background. He was also prevented from returning to the Supreme Court. So he opened the law school in Gilmer and occupied himself with it until the carpetbaggers left in 1874. Roberts returned to the Supreme Court then and went on to be elected governor in 1878.

Another Upshur County man named Roberts was up when Oran Roberts was down and down when Oran Roberts got back up. Meshack Roberts was a slave owned by O. B. Roberts of Gilmer. O. B. Roberts went away with the Confederate Army during the Civil War. Meshack kept O.B.'s plantation going and earned enough money working as a blacksmith to buy a little land for himself. Meshack had some trouble with the Ku Klux Klan during the Reconstruction era right after the war. O.B. sent him to Marshall to keep him from getting hurt. Meshack got active in politics and Methodist church affairs in Marshall and got elected to the Legislature. He founded Wiley College at Marshall in 1873 while he was up. Meshack lost his office and his status when Reconstruction ended, and he's believed to have moved away from the area around 1877. But Wiley College is still in business.

These are some of the historical markers in Upshur County:

- U.S. 271, five miles north of Gilmer, the Ben Phillips Place.
- U.S. 271, 11.6 miles south of Gilmer, the John O'Bryne Home.
- 400 N. Titus Street, Gilmer, site of a Confederate Hat Factory.

Lake Gladewater is in the southern end of Upshur County

2) In the 1820s the Cherokees blazed a trail through the wilderness later called The Cherokee Trace. It is described in this historical marker near the Upshur County Courthouse. 2

and the northern part of the city of Gladewater is in this county. The rest of the city is in Gregg County.

GREGG COUNTY

If Texas had a few more counties like Gregg County, the Arabs would be looking for somebody else to buy their oil. This one county has produced more than two and one half billion barrels of oil since 1931. No other county has produced as much.

Gregg County was organized in 1873. The county was named for General John Gregg of the Confederate Army. Gregg was in command of Hood's Texas Brigade when he was killed in battle in Virginia in 1864. Gregg was a native of Alabama and lived in Texas only briefly before the war.

The county seat of Gregg County is Longview. Much of the income here comes from oil and businesses serving the oil industry. But Longview is also a major manufacturing center. It is also the home of Le Tourneau College. The college was founded by R. G. Le Tourneau. He was the genius responsible for some of the most advanced earth-moving equipment. There is a Caddo Indian Museum between Highway 80 and Harrison Road in Longview, exhibiting some relics from the Indian and colonial days. It is open every day. There is no

1

1) Kilgore is understandably proud of its "forest of steel derricks." This marker tells how a single tract of a little more than one acre had produced, by 1966, more than two and a half million barrels of crude oil. The total today is far higher. 2) At one time, more than 1,000 oil derricks could be counted along Kilgore streets. Most of the derricks are gone now — but plenty of pumps are still working even in residential neighborhoods.

2

admission fee, but donations are encouraged. Longview Museum and Arts Center at 200 North Green Street is open weekdays and Saturday mornings. There is no admission charge.

The city nearest to the center of the East Texas Oilfield is Kilgore. It was founded in 1872 as a way station on the Missouri-Pacific Railroad. The oil was discovered in 1930. The population at the time was 590. Ten years later Kilgore had 6,700 people. City lots were bristling with derricks. There is an historical marker on one of those lots today proclaiming it the richest acre in the world. The marker is at Main and

3

3) Oil production quickly made Kilgore a boom town and a manufacturing center. The city commemorates its petroleum success with such attractions as this steel derrick with the lone star on top. 4) Another of Kilgore's noted attractions is the precision marching group called the Kilgore Rangerettes. They've been featured at parades and football games everywhere.

4

Commerce. There are more than 1100 producing wells within the Kilgore city limits. Part of the city is in Rusk County.

Kilgore is also famous for the Rangerettes. This precision marching group was founded and trained by Gussie Nell Davis of Kilgore College. The Rangerettes have been featured at football games, parades, fairs and festivals all over the world.

The Placid Oil Company of Dallas is now building an East Texas Oil Museum on the campus of the Kilgore College.

Gladewater is at the northwestern edge of Gregg County, and it spills over into Upshur County. Gladewater was started

1) The Gregg County Courthouse at Longview reflects the modern look of a county prospering from major petroleum reserves. The county produces nearly half a billion dollars worth of oil and gas every year.

at another site, and its original name was St. Clair. The town moved to the present location to get closer to the Texas and Pacific Railroad line. The name was changed to Gladewater because the site is on Glade Creek.

Gladewater may have the richest self-supporting cemetery in the world. There is a cemetery here with its own oil well, producing all the money it takes to keep up the cemetery and then some.

There is an old log cabin jail in Gladewater, at 303 South Center Street.

These are some of the other sites with historical markers in the Longview and Gregg County area:

- Fredonia Street at Tyler Street, Longview, site of the last raid of the Dalton gang.
- Brown-Birdsong Home, 104 North Whaley Street, Longview.
- Campbell-Salmon Home, 521 North 2nd Street, Longview.
- Dean-Kenner-Crim Place, 101 East Lantrip Street, Longview.
- F. L. Whaley House, 101 East Whaley Street, Longview.
- Flewellen-Eason Homestead, 206 South Center Street, Longview.
- Lacy-Womack home, 411 South Center Street, Longview.
- Old Campbell Home, 433 South Center Street, Longview.

Most of these places are not open to the public.

VAN ZANDT COUNTY

The earliest oxcart road from Shreveport to Dallas passed through the area that is now Van Zandt County. Interstate 20 and U.S. 80 both pass through the county today. But Van Zandt County retains the rural character it has always had.

2

3 *2) Van Zandt County got its courthouse and county government settled in Canton after a major dispute. 3-4) These photos give some flavor of the famous Canton "Trade Day" the way it was in the 1920s and the way it is today.* 4

Van Zandt County was created in 1848. The original county seat was a town called Sabine Lake, but the government was moved to Canton in 1850. County officials got excited when the Texas and Pacific Railroad started building a line through Wills Point. They wanted to move the county seat to Wills Point. The citizens of Canton armed themselves and marched on Wills Point to settle the dispute by force. The Texas Supreme Court intervened and ordered the county government to keep its seat at Canton. It has been here ever since. The present courthouse was built in 1937, and it has a 1930's look about it.

The institution known as "Canton Trade Day" has been flourishing in Canton since the 1870's. This event is also known as "First Monday." It was held on the first Monday of each month when it started. It has come to be concentrated during the weekend preceding the first Monday in each month

1

1) The big salt mine at Grand Saline makes Van Zandt County aware of the value of its salt deposits. This building was made — of blocks of salt — for the county's salt festival in 1977.

in recent years. The affair is usually finished and done with by Monday now. The Trade Day began as an occasion for settlers to get together and swap horses and livestock. Trading in other items developed over the years, and now the First Monday Trade Day at Canton is an outsized flea market. Some of the items offered here these days are reproductions, and buyers should be cautious. If there are any bargains to be had here, they probably will be had Sunday afternoons when traders will sometimes knock something off their prices to avoid having to pack up merchandise and haul it away. Some trading in coon dogs and horses and farm implements still goes on, and there are some things here you do not see everywhere, but the character of the event is unfortunately trending toward the typical 20th Century American Garage Sale.

One of the biggest salt mines in the United States is located at Grand Saline in Van Zandt County. The Caddo Indians had discovered the salt here before the first white settlers came in 1840. The first white settler was John Jordan, and he realized the value of what he had found. Jordan started working the salt deposits in 1845 with a couple of iron kettles he hauled in from Shreveport. There has been a commercial salt operation here ever since that time. Morton Salt Company is running the operation today. The company conducts no tours of the mine.

Van Zandt Company was named for Isaac Van Zandt. He came to East Texas from Mississippi in 1838 to practice law. Van Zandt served in the Congress of the Republic, and he helped work out the treaty that made Texas part of the United States. Van Zandt was campaigning for governor when he came down with yellow fever and died in Houston in 1847.

One of the oldest towns in Van Zandt County is Edom on Farm Road 314. Edom has been enjoying a little revival as a center for artisans and craftsmen of various kinds. There is an

2) The Coltharp-Beall House on Farm Road 279 near the Henderson County line, was built in 1849 by James Coltharp. It was used as a stagecoach stop. The first sermon preached in the area was preached here — and the building also once served as a post office. 3) This is a rough sketch of Chief Bowles of the Cherokees. He died in 1839 in a fight to avoid being forced out of Texas. The old chief was in his 80s, but made a gallant fight.

2

3

ancient stagecoach inn outside Edom on Farm Road 279 off U.S. 64 near the Henderson County line. It is known as the Coltharp-Beall House, built by settlers from Georgia in 1849.

Relations between the new Republic of Texas and the Cherokee Indians came to a melancholy end in this county in 1839. The Cherokees were in East Texas when the first white settlers came, but they had no place to call their own. They had been pushed out of the southeastern United States by white settlers. Sam Houston had known and worked with the Cherokees in Tennessee and in the Oklahoma Indian territory before he came to Texas. He trusted them, and they trusted him. The Cherokees in Texas had tried to get the Spanish to give them a land grant, but they never got anything more than informal permission to live in the area between the Neches and Sabine Rivers, north of the road to Nacogdoches. They

1

1) The old Roseland Plantation, between Tyler and Grand Saline, was decaying like many other 19th Century homes when Mrs. W. C. Windsor of Tyler got hold of it and began to make repairs. Today it looks much like it did before the Civil War when it was headquarters for a major plantation. 2) The Wills Cabin at Wills Point in Van Zandt County.

2

got nothing better from the Mexicans after Mexico won its independence. Sam Houston made a treaty with Chief Bowles of the Cherokees in the early days of the revolution. The treaty recognized the Cherokees' right to the lands they occupied. There is no reason to suppose Houston was insincere. But the Republic of Texas was just a dream when the treaty was made. When the dream came true, the Texas Senate refused to ratify the treaty. Houston served a term as President of the Republic, and then Mirabeau B. Lamar was elected President. Mexican agents were trying to get the Cherokees to make war on the Republic, and there were a few incidents. Texans got alarmed and wanted to be rid of the Cherokees. The Lamar government sent the Cherokees word they must leave Texas or be forced out. Chief Bowles was in his 80's by then. He was not personally inclined to make an issue of it. But his people thought they ought to fight, and the chief thought if they fought their chief had to fight with them. The

3

3) The T. Z. Woodhouse residence in Wills Point was built in 1872 with materials hauled by ox wagons from the ports of Jefferson and Shreveport. Woodhouse descendants still live here.

fight began in what is now Henderson County on July 15, 1839. It ended July 16 here in Van Zandt County, the way it was bound to end. Chief Bowles was killed, wearing a sash and sword Sam Houston had given him. The surviving Cherokees fled to the Indian territory that eventually became Oklahoma. The final clash occurred five miles east of Colfax, in Van Zandt County. You can picnic in the roadside park by the marker at the site on Interstate 20 where the Cherokees made their last stand. The forces of the Republic were led in this engagement by Thomas J. Rusk, Edward Burleson and Kelsey Douglas.

KAUFMAN COUNTY

Kaufman County was organized in 1848. It was named for D. S. Kaufman. He was a member of the House of Representatives when Texas was a Republic and he was elected to Congress when Texas was admitted to the Union. Kaufman was the first member from Texas ever to be seated in the U.S. House of Representatives.

The county seat is the city of Kaufman. The city was settled originally by Dr. William King, and it was known as Kingsboro until it was designated the county seat. There is a marker at 607 North Clay Street, where King built his original shelter. He called it King's Fort.

There were Caddo, Kickapoo, Delaware and Cherokee Indians living here when Dr. King and a small group of settlers

1

1) The modern Kaufman County Courthouse, built in 1956, is a far cry from the first Kaufman courthouse located in a remodeled blacksmith shop. 2) Dr. L. E. Griffith came to Texas in 1836 and one of his first patients was General Sam Houston. Houston needed treatment for the wound he suffered at the battle of San Jacinto. 3) Dr. Griffith's home in Terrell can be visited by appointment.

2

3

4

4) If you appreciate old houses, you should drive along Griffith Street in Terrell. A number of stately 19th Century homes are still standing here in a fine state of repair.

arrived about 1840. The Indians accepted the white settlers readily, and there was only one recorded instance of an Indian attack in this county.

The first courthouse in Kaufman was a remodeled blacksmith shop. The present courthouse was built in 1956.

There is some oil and gas in Kaufman County. Ranching is bigger than farming here. Several highways meet and cross at Kaufman. But Interstate 20 misses the county seat. It passes closer to Terrell at the northern end of the county. Terrell is three or four times as big as Kaufman. There is a state mental hospital at Terrell. Porter Farms on Farm Road 986 a mile north of Terrell was the site of the first joint U.S. and Texas Agricultural Experiment Station.

A medical doctor named L. E. Griffith moved to Texas from Maryland in 1836. He arrived here just in time to help take care of the wounds General Sam Houston suffered during the Battle of San Jacinto. Dr. Griffith and Houston became close friends and the doctor practiced medicine in the settlements at San Augustine, Nacogdoches and Milam before he came to Terrell. Griffith settled here in 1883 and lived here until he died in 1897. The doctor's home is open to visitors by appointment. The Terrell Chamber of Commerce

1

1) This well-preserved example of a simple and spacious early Texas home stands at 803 First Street in Terrell.

handles the appointments. The Griffith home is at 805 1st Street.

There are several other homes from the 80's and 90's in the 500 and 700 blocks of Griffith Street.

Railroad tycoon E. H. R. Green lived here when he was running the Texas Midland Railroad in the 1890's. The Texas Midland became part of the Southern Pacific. Green's private railroad business car is still here.

One of our governors once ran a newspaper here. Oscar Branch Colquitt was publishing a paper here when he got elected to the State Senate. Colquitt went on to serve in several other offices before he was elected governor in 1912. Colquitt left the Governor's Office in 1915 and in 1928 he was the leader of Texas Democrats for Herbert Hoover. It was one of those times when the Democrats were running a presidential candidate Texas Democrats did not like. The Democratic candidate that year was Al Smith. One of his problems

2) Matthew Cartwright obviously spared no expense to build this balconied mansion in Terrell. The builder was the son of the Matthew Cartwright who built one of the early showplaces in San Augustine. 2

was that he was a Catholic. That was a bigger problem in politics then than it is now.

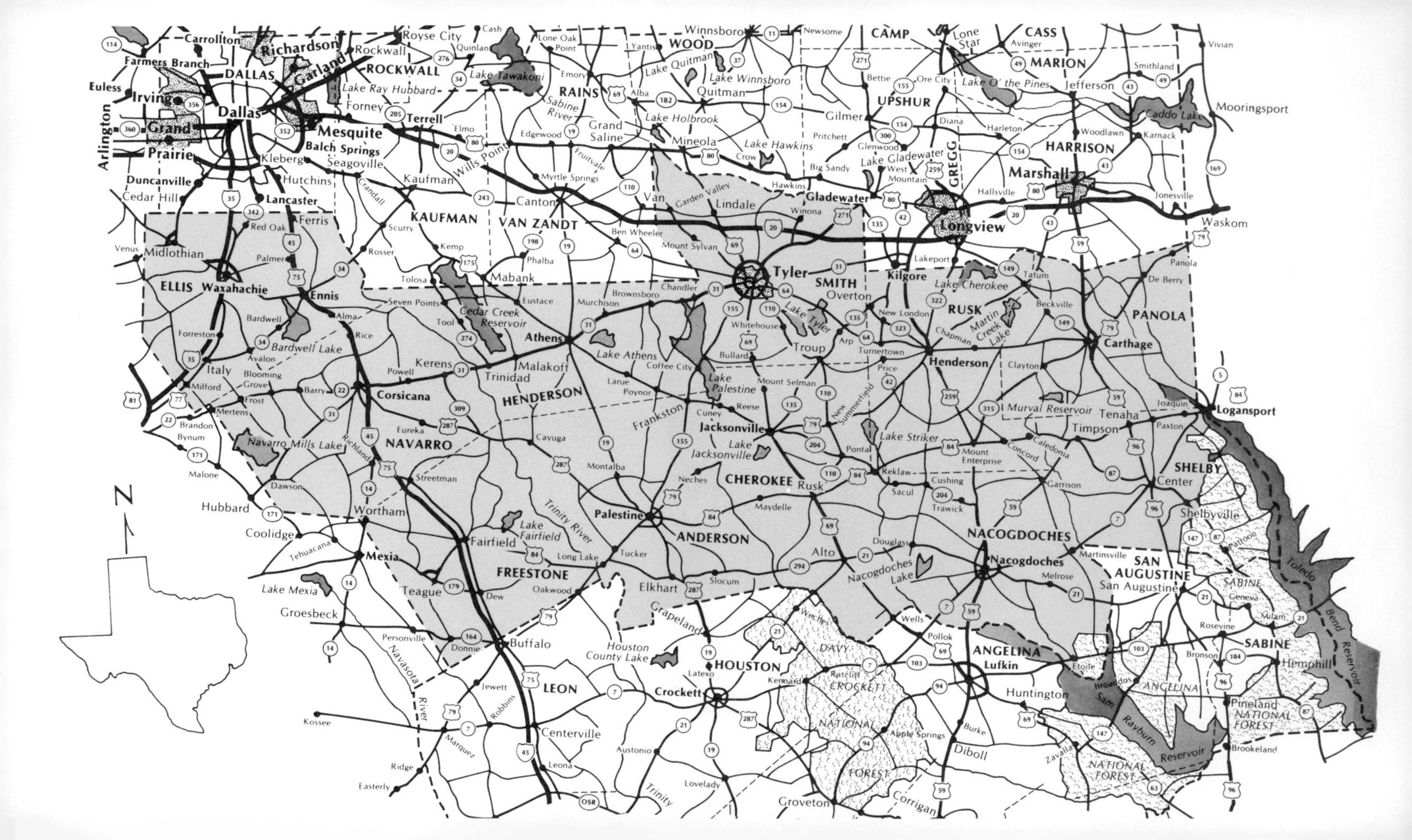

CASS
MARION
HARRISON
CAMP
UPSHUR
GREGG
WOOD
RAINS
ROCKWALL
DALLAS
KAUFMAN
VAN ZANDT
SMITH
RUSK
PANOLA
SHELBY
SAN AUGUSTINE
SABINE
NACOGDOCHES
ANGELINA
CHEROKEE
HOUSTON
ANDERSON
HENDERSON
ELLIS
NAVARRO
FREESTONE
LEON
Dallas
Grand Prairie
Arlington
Irving
Garland
Richardson
Mesquite
Balch Springs
Terrell
Kaufman
Canton
Tyler
Longview
Marshall
Kilgore
Gladewater
Henderson
Carthage
Logansport
Center
Nacogdoches
Lufkin
Jacksonville
Rusk
Palestine
Crockett
Athens
Corsicana
Waxahachie
Ennis
Fairfield
Mexia
Buffalo
Centerville
Lake Tawakoni
Lake Ray Hubbard
Lake O' the Pines
Caddo Lake
Cedar Creek Reservoir
Lake Tyler
Lake Palestine
Lake Athens
Navarro Mills Lake
Bardwell Lake
Lake Fairfield
Lake Mexia
Houston County Lake
Nacogdoches Lake
Lake Striker
Murval Reservoir
Toledo Bend Reservoir
Sam Rayburn Reservoir
Trinity River
Sabine River
Navasota River
SABINE NATIONAL FOREST
ANGELINA NATIONAL FOREST
DAVY CROCKETT NATIONAL FOREST
N

Athens and East Central Texas

Ellis, Henderson, Smith, Rusk, Panola,
Shelby, Nacogdoches, Cherokee, Anderson,
Navarro and Freestone Counties.

This section of the state includes some of the richest farmlands and some of the oldest settlements. It includes forests and oilfields and a grist mill and a steam railroad.

There are no interstate freeways in this area except for I-45 along the western edge. This is no disadvantage. The U.S. and State Highways and the Farm Roads are better than we have any right to expect.

Large sections of East Texas are legally dry. It takes a little time to find the local bootlegger. If you like a drink with your dinner, you may want to ask what the local rules are before you decide to make an overnight stop.

ELLIS COUNTY

It is quite likely that the major freeways between the major cities in Texas eventually will become continuous corridors of urban and industrial development. This blessing will fall upon Ellis County about as soon as it falls upon any county. Ellis County is directly south of Dallas County. Interstate 45 passes through it and Interstate 35 also passes through it. Waxahachie is on I-35. Ennis in on I-45. Both cities have some major industrial plants now. They will have many more.

Ellis County was organized in 1850. It was named for Richard Ellis. He was the chairman of the Convention of 1836 where the Texas Declaration of Independence was writ-

1

1) The Ellis County Courthouse is a good example of Texas Gothic architecture. It is a flamboyant product of the exuberant design styles of the 1890s. It is listed in the National Register of Historic Places, so it is apt to be around for a long time. It is built of granite and sandstone.

ten. He later served four terms in the Senate of the Republic.

There were Tonkawa, Kickapoo, Bidai, Anadarko and Waco Indians living in this area when the first white settlers came. The black land here is very rich. This was cotton country when the cotton business was at its height. Cotton made many Ellis County farmers rich in the 80's and 90's and the early 1900's. The farmers made the merchants and bankers rich and much of what the farmers and merchants and bankers built with their wealth is still here.

The county seat is Waxahachie. The name is one of the most often mispronounced in a state where a lot of place names are mispronounced. Waxahachie has nothing to do with wax, and the first syllable is not pronounced "wax". The first two "a"s are long . . . . like the "a"s in "AH-HAH". The third "a" is a short "a", as in "hatchet". It is an Indian word. The town was named for Waxahachie Creek. It means Buffalo Creek.

Waxahachie has had four courthouses. The present one was completed in 1896. It is sure to be preserved whenever the county has to build a new courthouse. This one is protected by the state law that gives some protection to all courthouses and it is also listed in the National Register of Historic Places. It is an outstanding example of what is sometimes called Texas Gothic.

The courthouse building cost $175,000 when a dollar was worth a dollar. It is made of Texas granite and sandstone. The contractor brought three stone carvers in from Italy to carve the decorations. The decorations include one very appealing female face and an assortment of male and female faces in varying degrees of ugliness. The story is that one of the stonecutters fell for his landlady's daughter. He supposedly carved the pretty face as a likeness of her when he thought she might find something interesting in him. She

2

3

4

Photos 2) and 3) tell the story of a stonecutter's disappointment. In 2) the landlord's daughter is portrayed as attractive. In 3) she is decidedly unattractive. 4) The "gingerbread" touches on many old homes like this Waxahachie residence, are carefully maintained since they are now expensive to replace.

never did, and the story is that he carved the ugly faces to express his general dissatisfaction with the town and its people after the landlady's daughter married somebody else. Makes an interesting story and an unusual building.

The National Register of Historic Places includes 25 square blocks of the city of Waxahachie in what it describes as the Ellis County Courthouse Historic District. The historic district includes more than 50 homes and buildings from the days of the cotton boom. Many of the old homes are decorat-

These old homes in Waxahachie explain the appeal of the city's historic district. It contains more than 50 homes and buildings that date from the cotton boom days. A Gingerbread Trail Tour of Homes is held each year, usually in June.

ed with the wood carving known as "gingerbread". The people of Waxahachie hold a Gingerbread Trail Tour of Homes once a year. It is usually in June, and some of the old gingerbread homes are open to visitors then. If you don't make it in June, you can see the exteriors of many of the old mansions by driving west on Main Street from the courthouse square to Grand Avenue. The Ellis County Historical Museum and Art

1

1) The kind of advertising that Americans knew in the 19th Century is still visible in the old Chautauqua Auditorium in Waxahachie. This old auditorium screen contains ads for all kinds of enterprises — some of them still in business here.

Gallery at 604 West Main is open Wednesdays and Sundays and there is no admission fee.

There is a park at the south end of Grand Avenue where the Chautauqua Society presented first rate speakers and entertainment every summer before radio and television. The park is Getzendaner park. The old Chautauqua building where William Jennings Bryan and Will Rogers once appeared has been restored. This building is also listed in the National Register of Historic Places. Farm families used to come to town and camp on the grounds around the Chautauqua Building during the two weeks when the programs were being presented.

Waxahachie has a restaurant that Esquire magazine has listed as one of the two dozen best eating places in the country. It is called Durham House. The address is 603 North Rogers Street. The building is an old home.

Ennis is not as old as Waxahachie. Ennis grew up around a way station on the Houston and Texas Central Railroad. That road reached here in 1871 on its way to Dallas. Ennis is the center of an area settled by farmers from Czechoslovakia. So Ennis is the site of the National Polka Festival. They have parades and dancing and plenty of Czech food here the first weekend in May every year.

There are six large parks around the Bardwell Reservoir, on State Highway 34 southwest of Ennis. There are some areas around Ennis where the bluebonnets are as thick and pretty in April as they are anywhere in the state. Highway 34 east of Ennis usually has some spectacular views during the bluebonnet season. The bluebonnets were here when the first white settlers came. The settlers started calling them bluebonnets because the flowers resemble the sunbonnets pioneer women wore. The plant is also called buffalo clover. But cows do not eat bluebonnets. The bluebonnet has been the state flower of Texas since 1901.

1

1) Athens is the county seat of Henderson County and the courthouse with its tall columns is in the Greek tradition. In this respect, it is similar to many courthouses in the South and Southwest. There was a great revival of interest in classical Greece and Rome in the later 19th Century. Many public buildings and many private homes wound up looking a little like ancient temples.

HENDERSON COUNTY

Henderson County was organized in 1846. It was named for the man occupying the Governor's office at that time. The man was James Pinckney Henderson. Governor Henderson served one really eventful term in the office. He was the first governor to be elected after Texas joined the Union. The Mexican War began shortly after Henderson took office, and he persuaded the Legislature to authorize him to go to Mexico to take personal command of the Texas troops fighting there. Henderson commanded the Second Texas Regiment at the Battle of Monterrey and became a major general in the U.S. Army. Henderson returned to the governor's office after the fighting ended, but he decided not to seek a second term. He went back to his law practice until 1857 when he was elected to the U.S. Senate.

Oil and gas are the principal sources of income here, but there is farming and ranching, too. And there have been potteries and brick factories here almost from the beginning. There is plenty of the right kind of clay in the soil here. A family named Cogburn from Georgia operated a pottery here from 1857 until 1866. M. K. Miller founded the Athens Pottery in 1885. Miller's father and grandfather were potters. He walked here from Dallas. His descendants are still making pots in Athens.

The county seat of Henderson County is the city of Athens. It was named for the capital of Greece or for the Athens in Georgia, depending upon which story you believe. The city was founded in 1850 specifically to be the county seat. The present courthouse was built in 1913.

2

2) James Pickney Henderson was not your ordinary governor. Soon after he took office in 1846, Henderson got a leave of absence to lead Texas troops in the Mexican War. Later he served in the U.S. Senate. 3) Lake Palestine is one of Henderson County's most popular recreation areas.

3

Black-eyed peas are grown and eaten all over East Texas, but Athens claims to be the black-eyed pea capital of the world. There is a Black-Eyed Pea Jamboree here every July. Black-eyed peas have not made any tremendous impression in gourmet circles. But plenty of East Texas cooks know how to make them tasty. They can be bought in cans or frozen, but a serious East Texas cook will start with dried peas or peas fresh from the garden. What is done with them depends upon whether they are dried or fresh. This recipe for fresh black-

1

2

3

1) Historic markers in this Athens park commemorate the beginnings of the county's commercial pottery industry. 2) This marker shows where Athens' first factory was. 3) Here is a tense moment in Athens' annual black-eyed pea shelling contest.

eyed peas has been used by one East Texas family for three generations:

Using fresh peas (2 quarts of peas)

1. Shell and wash peas in pan and drain off water.
2. Using clean pan, pour in peas and add small amount of clean water (only enough water to keep the peas from burning; the water should not cover the peas).
3. Place pan on stove; turn burner on low heat.
4. Let peas simmer for about 20 minutes and stir slowly every now and then.
5. Have a pan of hot water ready. When peas have sim-

4

4) The Old Fiddlers contest in Athens each May draws a lot of young fiddlers as well, and crowds come from some distance to hear them. 5) Not many old grist mills are still running but this one is operating pretty much as it did a century ago. It is at Poyner, southeast of Athens.

5

mered for 20 minutes, pour hot water into pan of peas.

6. Cut about one-half pound of smoke jowl or cured bacon into small chunks. Put the meat into pan of peas and stir.
7. Add one tablespoon of sugar and salt to taste.
8. Turn burner to medium heat and bring peas to a medium boil.
9. It is not necessary to cover pan, but it is a good idea.
10. Cook peas for 1½ to 2 hours, stirring slowly every now and then.

People didn't start growing black-eyed peas because they were crazy about eating them. They started eating them because they were easy to grow and they learned how to make them palatable because they didn't have a whole lot of choice. There is a story that eating black-eyed peas on New Year's Day brings good luck for the year. The story may have been started by an East Texas mother trying to get her family to eat the peas.

1

1) Near the community of Malakoff in Henderson County some ancient stone heads caused considerable archaelogical excitement when they were discovered back in the 1930s. This marker is near the site on State Highway 31, not far from Trinidad.

Athens also stages a contest for fiddlers every year on the last weekend in May. They call it the Old Fiddlers' Contest, but fiddlers do not have to be old to enter. Thousands of visitors come to hear the fiddlers play on the courthouse square.

There are some artifacts from a pioneer Athens factory on display in the J. Pinckney Henderson Park, on State Highway 315, eight miles south of the courthouse.

There is a marker at the site of the pioneer pottery, eight blocks south of the courthouse, in Athens.

There is a marker at Chandler, in the northeast corner of the county, two-tenths of a mile east of the Chandler Post Office, noting that three generations of the Yarborough family have lived in the same house here. Ralph Yarborough was born here, and it was here he took his first oath of office as United States Senator on January 1, 1959. The Senator's father was Justice of the Peace here. Chandler also has a marker noting that Chandler is the place where the final battle between the soldiers of the Republic of Texas and Chief Bowles' Cherokees began. The battle ended in Van Zandt County when Chief Bowles was killed.

There is a grist mill still grinding corn and selling corn meal in this county. It is on U.S. 175 at Poyner southeast of Athens. Oochie Dickerson operates the mill pretty much the way it operated one hundred years ago, except that he is not using water power. He operates on the honor system. If he is away, you can take a bag of meal and leave the money in a box he keeps for that purpose.

A stone head carved by some early Indians was found in a gravel pit near Trinidad in 1929. Similar heads were found in

2

2) Dr. E. H. Sellards stands in the pit where the Malakoff relics were found. Two of the heads are at left. The heads apparently were carved by Indians in prehistoric times.

1935 and 1939 in the same area. Fossilized remains of prehistoric horses and camels and elephants have been found in the same area and archaeologists believe the heads were carved thousands of years ago. The mysterious early residents are called Malakoff Man because the relics were found near the community of Malakoff. There is a marker near the site, at the western city limits of Trinidad on State Highway 31. The original sandstone head found here in 1929 is now in the Texas Memorial Museum in Austin.

There were rumors in the early days of a silver mine on Cat Creek in the Malakoff area. The rumor's never been confirmed, but there are deposits of lignite and clay here.

SMITH COUNTY

The United States Congress has been talking off and on for years about naming a national flower. The marigold is a sentimental favorite because it was sponsored for years by the late Senator Everett Dirksen, and anything described by him sounded like a good idea. But more people favor the rose. If the Congress ever decides to make the rose the national flower, there will be a question about which rose. The Congressmen may have to call for samples from Smith County before they resolve that question. There are hundreds of varieties, and they are all here.

Roses began to be cultivated commercially in Smith County around 1875. Roses were a major industry here by the early

1 *1) Tyler is the Rose Capital of the World and the city's rose garden has more than 500 varieties blooming much of the time. Crowds of rose lovers attend the annual Tyler Rose Festival here every October.*

1900's, and Tyler has been known as the Rose Capital of the World ever since.

Smith County was organized in 1846. The county was named for General James Smith. He came to Texas from South Carolina in 1835 and fought in the revolution. He reached the rank of colonel during the revolution and became a brigadier general in command of the Republic's troops on the northwest frontier in 1841. Smith was representing Rusk County in the Legislature when the Legislature decided to establish this county, and his fellow lawmakers decided to name the new county for him.

Tyler is the county seat. It was settled in the early 1840's and named for President John Tyler of the United States. The present courthouse was built in 1955. Tyler is an important manufacturing and trading center, and there is substantial oil production here. But the name Tyler means roses to most people, and they will not see anything in Tyler to make them think differently. The Tyler Municipal Rose Garden is the biggest rose garden in the nation. Visitors are welcome and there is no admission charge. The garden has thousands of rose bushes. There are more than 500 different varieties here. The annual Tyler Rose Festival is held in October. But there are roses in bloom here most of the time. The Municipal Rose Garden is next to the Fairground, on State Highway 31, at Fair Park Drive.

Tyler has an Azalea and Spring Flower Show in late March and early April, too. Several Tyler homes are open to visitors then, and the redbuds and dogwoods usually are in bloom. A marker in a pleasant roadside park on U.S. 271 just north of

2

2) Smith County's fairly modern courthouse in Tyler was built in 1955. The county has benefited from oil production, tourism and a sizable community of affluent retired people. 3) One of the restored early homes in Tyler is the Loftin-Wiggins House at 610 North Bois D'Arc.

3

the 323 Loop designates this as the place where the Confederate government maintained a big camp for prisoners of war during the Civil War. There was a big stockade. As many as 6,000 prisoners were held here at Camp Ford in very primitive conditions. Most of the prisoners were captured Union soldiers. But Confederate deserters and Union sympathizers were held here, too. This was plantation country. The residents here had a style of living that was similar to that in the Old South and sentiment in areas like this was strongly in

1

1) One of the best-known historic homes in Tyler is on the city's main thoroughfare. The Goodman LeGrand House on North Broadway was built after the Civil War by a Confederate veteran. It is now a museum. 2) This roadside park is on US 271 north of Tyler. Its picnic shelters are built to resemble oil derricks, in keeping with the area's position in the oil industry.

2

favor of the Confederate cause. But it was never unanimous. In some parts of the state, there were as many Union sympathizers as Southern sympathizers, or more. You will not find this fact carved on the Confederate monuments around the state. Camp Ford was destroyed by the Union occupying force after Appomattox. It was probably about the first thing they did.

An old home at 624 North Broadway in Tyler has been turned into a museum. The displays include artifacts from the Caddo Indian days and the colonial and Civil War periods. The building is called the Goodman Le Grand Home. It was built by a bachelor Confederate officer named Gallatin Smith. It is open daily, and there is no admission charge.

The Tyler Museum of Art is open every day except Monday, and it is free, too. The Museum of Art is at 1300 South Mahon Avenue.

The Tyler State Park is in the forest about 10 miles north of

3) Tyler State Park is 10 miles north of the city. Nearby is Bellwood Lake with provisions for water sports of all kinds. 3

the city on Park Road 16, off Farm Road 14. This is a Class I Park with provisions for camping and picnicking, hiking, fishing, swimming and boating. There are 119 campsites. You might get one without a reservation, but you'd be better off making reservations with the Park Superintendent, Tyler State Park, Route 9, Tyler 75701. The admission fee of $1.00 per vehicle applies unless you have an annual permit or parklands passport. This is an old park. It was built by the Civilian Conservation Corps in the early 1930's.

A Tyler man named Bryan Garrett has accumulated a collection of old railroad cars and railroad relics on his whistle-stop ranch just south of Flint. He hopes to make a museum out of this collection some day. The place is not actually open to the public in the meantime. But Garrett is reasonably tolerant of other railroad buffs.

RUSK COUNTY

Rusk County was organized in 1843 and named for Thomas Jefferson Rusk. He was one of the leading lights in the Texas Revolution. Rusk was organizing volunteers to fight the Mexicans as early as 1835. He was one of the signers of the Declaration of Independence and Secretary of War in the Interim Government. He was at San Jacinto and was one of the commanders of the forces that expelled the Cherokee

1

1) Thomas Jefferson Rusk was one of the movers and shakers of the early Texas Republic. He was noted as both soldier and lawyer. He played an active role in the battles and political maneuvers that led, ultimately, to Texas becoming a state. Rusk then served in the U.S. Congress. 2) The Old Birdwell House is 12 miles east of Mt. Enterprise on US 84, then one mile north.

2

Indians from Texas. Rusk served in the Congress of the Republic, and later, he and Sam Houston were the first two senators Texas sent to the Congress of the United States after annexation. Senator Rusk killed himself at his home in Nacogdoches in 1857 shortly after his wife died.

It was the custom of the Congress of the Republic and the Legislature of the state of Texas to locate the county seat as close as possible to the center of the county when a new county was established. This is how the county seat of Rusk County came to be situated where it is. It is the center of the county. And it was named Henderson in honor of J. Pinckney Henderson. He had not made it to the Governor's office at that time, but he was working to warm up the United States Congress to the idea of annexing Texas. The people in the new county of Rusk apparently thought he was a comer.

The city of Henderson grew fairly quickly during its first 20 years. But a big fire destroyed the courthouse and most of the

3

3) C. M. "Dad" Joiner hit it big in 1930 when he drilled his third well near Henderson after two dry holes. Joiner's "Daisy Bradford #3" ushered in the huge East Texas Oil Field. 4) This is the Daisy Bradford #7, at Joinerville, still producing after many years.

4

business district in 1860. The present courthouse was built in 1928.

A wildcatter from Oklahoma decided in 1930 that there ought to be oil under Henderson County. Some expert geologists thought otherwise. But Columbus Marvin "Dad" Joiner started drilling eight miles west of Henderson. He drilled two dry holes with his primitive rig. He borrowed some money and started a third well, and he put himself in the history books for all time. That well was the "Daisy Bradford Number 3". Joiner had discovered the East Texas Oil Field. There is a marker at the site of the discovery well, on State Highway 64, six miles west of Henderson. There is a replica of Joiner's derrick in Pioneer Park on U.S. 64 just west of Joinerville.

1) Monte Verdi Plantation was built in the 1840s and restored in 1967. 2) This marker memorializes the students and teachers killed in the explosion of the New London school in 1937. 3) The Howard Dickinson House is on South Main in Henderson.

The Rusk County Heritage Association maintains a museum in an old home at 501 South Main Street in Henderson. This is the oldest brick home in the county. It was built in 1855 and restored in 1967. It is known as the Howard-Dickinson House. The exhibits include historical items and period furnishings. There is an admission charge.

An old plantation home built in the 1840's has been restored in southern Rusk County. The plantation is Monte Verdi. It was originally the property of J. S. Devereux. He had 10,000 acres and a great many slaves. The plantation

4

4) This courthouse was the pride and joy of Carthage in Panola County for many years after it was built in 1885. But 65 years later county officials decided to replace it. There was considerable controversy over the decision. But the county officials won out and tore the old building down in the 1950s.

house was almost a ruin when the E. F. Lowrys of Texas City bought it and restored it. The place is not open to the public, but you can see it from the road. The road is a country road that runs west off Farm Road 2753 just north of U.S. 84.

A memorial marker at New London in northwestern Rusk County recalls that 286 students and teachers were killed in an explosion on March 18, 1937. The explosion was caused by a leak in the line supplying the New London School with natural gas. It destroyed the school.

There is a big new electric generating plant off State Highway 43 between Henderson and Tatum in northeastern Rusk County. It is one of the plants designed to burn lignite. There is a small new state park on the shores of the reservoir at the plant. It is called Martin Creek Park. There are provisions for fishing and launching boats and not much more.

PANOLA COUNTY

Panola County was established in 1846. The name is said to be an Indian word for cotton. The county seat is Carthage. A settlement named Pulaski was the original county seat. The county government moved to Carthage in 1848.

A picturesque courthouse was built on the square here in 1885. County officials were dissatisfied with the building by the 1950's. There was opposition to the idea of tearing down the old building with the turrets all around it, and some controversy. But the building eventually was torn down. The new courthouse was built in 1954 a few blocks off the square. The original square is now a park with a little gazebo. A courthouse very similar to the one Panola County destroyed in 1954 is still in use in Shelby County.

The old county jail building on the courthouse square in

2

1

1) This is Panola County's new courthouse at Carthage. 2) Devoid of prisoners or guards, the old Panola County Jail stands deserted on the courthouse square in Carthage. It was built in 1891. 3) This granite marker is a reminder of the time in 1840 when Texas was an independent republic and the marker proclaimed the boundary between the U.S. and Texas. It is located about 30 miles southeast of Carthage on Farm Road 31. It is about four feet high.

3

Carthage was a museum for a while. But the museum is no longer operating. The building is vacant.

Country entertainer Jim Reeves was born in Panola County, and he is buried in a cemetery on U.S. 79 about four miles west of downtown Carthage. Reeves was killed in a plane crash in 1964. His memorial includes a sidewalk in the form of a guitar and a statue.

Highway workers in 1971 found an old marker here that goes back to the days of the Republic. The marker is a block of granite, six inches square and four feet high. It sits on the boundary between Texas and Louisiana. It was the boundary between the United States and the Republic of Texas when the marker was put here. The letters U.S. appear on the east face of the marker, and the letters R.T. appear on the west face.

4) Lake Murvaul is a major recreation area 10 miles southwest of Carthage in Panola County. It covers a surface area of 3,820 acres. 4

The boundary here is the 32nd parallel. The marker is about 30 miles southeast of Carthage on Farm Road 31.

There are several resorts and marinas around Lake Murvaul in the southwestern corner of Panola County. Farm Road 1971 crosses the lake. They say the bass fishing is good here.

SHELBY COUNTY

Shelby County was established in 1836 and named for Isaac Shelby. He was one of the heroes of the American Revolution. The county includes a large part of the Sabine National Forest. The Toledo Bend Reservoir forms the county's eastern boundary.

There is some oil and gas production here, but the county's income is mostly from farming, ranching and poultry and from hunters and fishermen.

The county seat is the town of Center. The town was founded in 1866. They called it Center because it was in the center of the county. But it was not always the county seat. Shelbyville was the original county seat here. The present courthouse in Center was built in 1885 to replace an earlier courthouse destroyed by fire in 1882. This one was built by an Irish contractor named Gibson. He built it to resemble a castle he remembered in the old country. It is said to be the

1

1) The Shelby County Courthouse at Center is remarkably similar to the one (page 115) torn down by Panola County. This one is still standing and completely paid for.

only courthouse in the country of this design. But it looks like a twin to the courthouse Panola County tore down in the 1950's. The Shelby County Courthouse was finally paid for in 1978, 93 years after it was built. The county got way behind with its bills during the depression of the 1930's. There was money still due on the courthouse and on roads and on various other projects. The county's creditors went to Federal court and got an order consolidating all the debts and requiring the county to pay to the creditors the first $5,000 of taxes collected every year until the debt was paid off. The last payment was paid in 1978. Shelby County owns its courthouse.

There was quite a lot of rivalry in the early days among towns contending for the right to be the county seat. The decision to move the Shelby County seat from Shelbyville to Center was very unpopular in Shelbyville. People there decided they would not abide by it. But R. L. Parker of Center went to Shelbyville in the middle of the night with a couple of helpers and they gathered up all the county records and moved them to Center and mounted a watch over them. It worked, and Center has been the county seat ever since.

The courthouse was built with a secret passageway to allow the judge to slip out of the courtroom and leave the building without having to confront people made unhappy by his decisions.

This area was part of what was called "The Neutral Ground" during the days of Spanish and Mexican rule. The Spanish and Mexicans tried to prevent settlers from the

2

2) A kind of civil war broke out in Shelby County in the 1840s and it went on for several years before troops of the Republic of Texas restored order. The marker shows where the last "battle" took place. 3) Judy's Wood Shop in Shelby County sells barrels of all kinds. Judy's husband is a specialist in barrel staves for wine casks.

3

United States from occupying land within 20 leagues of the Louisiana border. They figured they would have trouble with those people trying to annex themselves to the United States. They were right, of course.

Settlers moved in, anyway. They had no official status so they largely took care of their own affairs and made their own rules. They grew accustomed to this arrangement, and they resented the efforts the government of the Republic made to establish a system of civil administration after the Revolution succeeded in 1836. Some of the old settlers formed themselves into an armed force and called themselves "Regulators." They intended to regulate what they regarded as interference with their system of vigilante justice. The supporters of the Republic's efforts to bring the area under an official system of administration formed an armed vigilante group of their

1 *1) R. Z. Wooten shows one of the buggies he has restored at his buggy shop near Timpson in Shelby County. Wooten is a retired carpenter now very busy with a second career.*

own. These people called themselves "Moderators." The clashes they had came to be called the "Regulator-Moderator War." There was some shooting, and there were several summary hangings, and the territory was kept in turmoil for about four years until President Sam Houston sent in the militia. He had the leaders of the two sides arrested. They were brought together and commanded to sign a peace treaty. Things were more peaceful after that.

A marker one mile south of Shelbyville on U.S. 59 proclaims this the site of the first battle in the "Regulator-Moderator War." The last battle was fought three miles northwest of Shelbyville. There is another marker there.

There is an entrance to the Sabine National Forest 11 miles southeast of Center on U.S. 87. The recreation areas in the park readily accessible from here are the Boles Field Area, seven miles east of Shelbyville by way of Farm Road 417 and Farm Road 2694, and the Ragtown Area, on Toledo Bend Reservoir, 15 miles southeast of Shelbyville by way of State Highway 87, Farm road 139 and Forest Service Roads 101 and 1262.

A retired carpenter named R. Z. Wooten keeps busy restoring old wagons and buggies at his place right outside the community of Timpson in northwest Shelby County. Wooten buys old relics and restores them and sells them. He says he will not restore old wagons and buggies for other people, but he might buy your old one and sell you one he has restored. He seems to be doing what he's doing more because he wants to than because he needs to.

2) You would not know that Nacogdoches is one of the most historic cities in Texas from its courthouse. The Nacogdoches County Courthouse was built in 1959 along ranch house lines. 2

NACOGDOCHES COUNTY

Nacogdoches calls itself the oldest town in Texas. It is the center of one of the most historic areas in the state.

This is one of the original counties established by the First Congress of the Republic in 1836. The town of Nacogdoches became the county seat. It was already an old town, with a long history of being the center of governmental and revolutionary activity. Few places anywhere have been involved in more revolutionary sallies and uprisings.

The area got its name long before it became a county. The name was the name of a tribe of Caddo Indians found living here in the early days of Spanish settlement. The Indians' main village was about where the city of Nacogdoches is now, and several Indian mounds have been found within the city limits.

Many cities have paved over the brick streets built in the early days of the automobile era. But the brick surfaces still show in Nacogdoches. They help define the town's character. The courthouse does not. It was built in 1959. It resembles a west Texas country club more than it resembles a courthouse.

The French explorer LaSalle may have been the first European to set foot here. That would have been about 1687 after the Frenchman mistook a Texas bay for the mouth of the Mississippi. LaSalle did a lot of walking, trying to find the Mississippi, before his men killed him. The French explorer Louis St. Denis was indirectly responsible for the establishment of the first Spanish outpost here. The French governor of Louisiana sent St. Denis into the Spanish territory of Texas

1 *1) The Old Stone Fort in Nacogdoches is a relic from the 18th Century. Its present location on the Stephen F. Austin University campus is its third location since it was first built.*

to see about getting some trade started. St. Denis set out from Natchitoches and made it to Mexico City. He got the Spanish viceroy interested in trade. The viceroy sent one of his captains and a small party back with St. Denis with instructions to establish an outpost on the Louisiana frontier. The Spaniards established a presidio and six Indian missions and the Spanish captain's daughter married Louis St. Denis. The settlement that became the city of Nacogdoches grew up around the Mission Nuestra Senora de Guadalupe de los Nacogdoches. The settlement was abandoned between 1718 and 1721 and again between 1762 and 1779. A Spaniard named Gil Ybarbo led a party of settlers back here in 1779, and there has been a settlement here continuously ever since. Ybarbo reputedly built the stone house that came to be known as the Old Stone Fort. This building now stands on the grounds of the Stephen F. Austin State University. It was rebuilt here in 1936 by the Texas Centennial Commission, and it is now a museum with exhibits recalling some of the history of this area. The museum is open every day, and it is free. The address is College at Griffith.

The Stone Fort originally stood on the square at Fredonia and Main Street. A drug company tore the original building down in 1902 in order to build a new drug store on the site. The materials were used to build a museum on the square and then the Centennial Commission came along in 1936 and bought that building and used the original materials to rebuild the Stone Fort where it is today.

2

2) This building on the campus of Nacogdoches High School is all that remains of the old Nacogdoches University, which flourished in the mid-19th Century. This building was completed in 1859.

Gil Ybarbo probably designed the building to serve mostly as a trading post and storehouse. But the Stone Fort at Nacogdoches has seen more duty as a fort than most of the Texas buildings that were designed to be forts. The building was a headquarters for the Gutierrez-McGee Expedition in 1812, and it was a base for the James Long Expedition in 1819. Both those expeditions ostensibly were intended to help the Mexicans run off the Spanish. Both probably were actually expressions of the United States' continuing interest in taking over the territory. The Philip Nolan Expedition probably was, too. Nolan came through here with a party of men in 1800, ostensibly to catch wild horses for sale in the United States. Suspicious Spanish troops killed Nolan and captured the other members of his party. The captured men were locked up in the old Stone Fort for several weeks before they were shipped south. One of the captives was Peter Bean, and he made another appearance here a little later in another role.

The later Gutierrez-McGee and Long Expeditions enjoyed some temporary successes. The Gutierrez-McGee party captured San Antonio and Long proclaimed a Republic. But the Spanish defeated and scattered the Gutierrez-McGee Expedition in 1813 and drove most of the Long Expedition back across the border in 1819. Dr. Long made another sally into Texas in 1821, and he was captured and later killed. This made a widow of Jane Long, but she joined Stephen F. Austin's colony of settlers and played a substantial role in Texas history.

1) Millard's Crossing in Nacogdoches is the handiwork of former Congresswoman Lera Thomas. She restored a group of early Texas buildings and added a museum and Texana collection.

The Mexicans won their independence from Spain in 1821, and the new Mexican government took over Nacogdoches. An Anglo settler named James Dill became the alcalde. The Stone Fort became a center of strife again when two brothers named Edwards got crossways with the Mexican government. Haden and Benjamin Edwards had an empresario contract with the government entitling them to bring settlers into the area. Some of the land included in their contract had already been claimed much earlier by Spanish families. The early settlers refused to leave, and the Mexican government took their side. Benjamin Edwards seized the Stone Fort and announced that he was proclaiming the independence of what he called the "Fredonia Republic." He thought other settlers would side with him, but they sided with the Mexican authorities instead and that was the end of the Fredonian Republic.

A significant prelude to the revolution occurred here in 1832. Settlers down south at Anahuac had just forced the removal of an unpopular Mexican administrator. Jose de las Piedras was the commander at Nacogdoches, and he got concerned that the settlers might try the same thing on him. He ordered all the settlers to turn in their arms. They refused to do it and demanded that Piedras declare in favor of the reform movement then being led by Santa Anna in Mexico. He refused to do that, and the settlers attacked his troops. Piedras and Company withdrew toward San Antonio and then surrendered. Piedras was removed from his command. Peter Bean was moved up from his post at Fort Teran to command the Mexican garrison at Nacogdoches. Many people believe the removal of Piedras helped make the Texas revolu-

2

2) The Old Stagecoach Inn at Chireno was a welcome sight to stage travelers rolling through Nacogdoches County in the 1840s. It was built on the Spanish route called El Camino Real, now Texas State Highway 21.

tion possible. Bean had come to the area originally with Philip Nolan's expedition. He became a Mexican citizen after he was captured. He was an officer in the Mexican Army, but he was reputed to be friendly with Sam Houston. Nacogdoches was a major gateway for American volunteers coming in to help Texas win independence.

Nacogdoches also figured in the Cordova Rebellion against the Republic of Texas. This uprising was engineered by a Mexican settler named Vicente Cordova. He persuaded some Cherokee Indians to help him overthrow the new Republic. He gathered up a party of Mexicans and Indians and took over an island in the Angelina River in August of 1838. Cordova announced that he and his followers were seceding from the Republic. The troops of the Republic attacked the rebels and scattered them. Chief Bowles of the Cherokees claimed that he had nothing to do with the Cordova enterprise, but the episode hastened the Republic's decision to expel the Cherokees.

The history of the Nacogdoches area is preserved in four other museums besides the Stone Fort:

The Old University Building on the campus of Nacogdoches High School. This is the only remaining building of the Nacogdoches University. It was completed in 1859. The exhibits include period furnishings and various historical displays. The museum is open daily during the summer months and by appointment the rest of the year. There is no admission charge.

1

1) The Roland Jones House in Nacogdoches is an example of what can be done to restore a splendid old house from the Victorian period to usefulness in the 20th Century. The home at 141 North Church St. is now a doctor's office.

Millard's Crossing Antiques and Texana Museum is a collection of old buildings and furnishings at 6020 North Street. Mrs. Lera Thomas put the collection together and restored the buildings. Mrs. Thomas is the widow of Congressman Albert Thomas and a former member of Congress herself. There are guided tours at Millard's Crossing daily at 9:30 a.m. and 2:00 p.m. and at 2:00 p.m. on Sundays. You can write to Mrs. Thomas at the North Street address, zip code 75961 or call her at 713-564-6969.

The Hoya Memorial Library and Museum is housed in the home the Adolphus Sterne family built about 1830. Sterne was once locked up by the Mexicans in the old Stone Fort. That was because he sided with the Edwards' brothers in their Fredonian Rebellion. He was also an early friend and supporter of Sam Houston. Sterne was a merchant, and he built his home with a store in one end. This place is really more library than museum, but there are some of Sam Houston's personal belongings on display here.

The Hoya Memorial Library and Museum is at 211 South Lanana Street and open daily except Sundays. There is no admission charge.

The Halfway House at Chireno is an old stagecoach inn built in the 1840's on what was then one of the principal roads in Texas. This was the Camino Real laid out by the Spanish Governor Domingo Teran in 1691. It is now Texas State Highway 21. Chireno is between Nacogdoches and San Augustine. The Halfway House is right on the highway. There is a small admission fee when it is open. It is an interesting old building just viewed from the outside when it is closed.

There are about 50 historical markers in and around Nacogdoches. Nearly a dozen of them are in the Oak Grove Cemetery on Lanana Street at Hospital Street. Thomas Jefferson Rusk and many other Texas heroes and pioneers are buried here.

2

2) Only one family lived at Rusk when the place was selected to be the county seat of Cherokee County. That was in 1846. Today, Rusk has a population exceeding 4,000. It is an important shipping point for the area's industry, farms and ranches.

There is no marker recalling that Moses Rose lived in Nacogdoches for a while after he accepted William Travis' famous offer and left the Alamo before the final assault and slaughter.

The first oil well drilled in Texas was near Nacogdoches. They named the place Oil Springs, but it never was a boom town. There was not that much oil. There is a marker at the site, and the tank is reputed to be the first metal oil tank in the state. The site is on a hiking trail that begins near the Community of Woden, southeast of Nacogdoches, off State Highway 21 and Farm Road 226.

Most of the records accumulated by the Spanish and Mexican authorities in the early days of the settlement at Nacogdoches were seized by Texas officials after San Jacinto. The originals are now in the State Archives in Austin. There are copies on file at the University of Texas at Austin and at the Stephen F. Austin University here in Nacogdoches.

It has been claimed that the first newspaper in Texas was printed here in 1813. But the Gaceta de Tejas probably was printed in Louisiana after the type was set here. The paper advocated independence from Spain, and there apparently was only one issue. A copy is on display in the Stone Fort Museum.

Many of the old homes in Nacogdoches are open for tours during the Homes and Historical Places Tour, usually in late April.

The southeastern corner of Nacogdoches County reaches the northern shores of Lake Sam Rayburn. The Army Engineers have more than a dozen parks around the lake. All of them have free boat ramps and four or five of them have marinas and campgrounds operated by concessionaires.

CHEROKEE COUNTY

This is the part of the state the Cherokee Indians occupied.

1

1) One of the oldest and best-preserved of the historic homes in Rusk is the Gregg Home on 4th Street.

Sam Houston promised them they could stay here. The last home of Cherokee Chief Bowles was in this county. The Indians gave their name to the county. They were driven out of Texas by troops led by Thomas Jefferson Rusk. He gave his name to the county seat. Rusk is the county seat of Cherokee County. The present courthouse was built in 1941. The actual final battle between the Texans and Cherokees took place in Henderson and Van Zandt counties, and there are more details in the chapters dealing with those counties.

The Cherokees were immigrants here themselves. The natives were the Caddo and Hasanai Indians. The first Europeans here were Spanish missionaries ministering to those Indians.

One of the early Texas experiments with trying to make prisons support themselves occurred here. A prison was built at Rusk and a foundry was included. The foundry was to make pig iron and pipe for the various state agencies from ore mined in the area. The state built a railroad to haul ore from Palestine to the foundry at Rusk. This arrangement continued until 1918 when the prison at Rusk was closed and converted to a mental hospital. Some of the old prison buildings are still doing duty at the hospital today. And the little railroad has been reborn.

The Texas Parks and Wildlife Department has put the tracks back in shape. The department has rounded up some antique steam locomotives and some old passenger cars and restored them. The department is operating tourist excursions between Palestine and Rusk. New depots have been built at

2) The Age of Steam is alive and well in Cherokee County since the Texas Parks and Wildlife Department has rebuilt the old railroad between Palestine and Rusk. The train is very popular and you'd better make reservations in advance. 3) Dr. I. K. Frazier built his home in Rusk in the 1850s. He was a noted early physician here.

3

each end of the line. The depots are surrounded by parks, and there is plenty of parking space. Passengers can buy tickets for the round trip or just one way. The fare is $5.75 for adults and $3.25 for children, round trip. The one way fares are $3.00 for adults and $1.75 for children. The round trip takes about three and a half hours. The old trains travel only about 20 miles an hour. The tracks wind through the forest, crossing several small streams and one river. This is one of the most popular attractions the Parks Department operates. The train is usually sold out completely. You should make reservations in advance. The phone number is 214-683-2561. You can see the train from a few points along U.S. 84 between Rusk and Palestine.

Eastern promoters got excited about the ore in East Texas in the late 1880's. They formed a company called the New Birmingham Iron and Improvement Company of Texas, and built a town and a couple of blast furnaces just south of Rusk near the present U.S. Highway 69. They got it started, and

1

2

3

1) Rusk didn't build the "world's longest footbridge" just to get in the record books. It was to help citizens back in the 1860s to get from one end of Rusk to the other in the rainy season. 2) and 3) show what happens during the Jacksonville rodeo in midsummer.

they were making iron. But there was a financial panic in 1893 and the Texas Legislature passed a law discouraging outside investment, and the company's biggest furnace was damaged by fire all about the same time. So New Birmingham did not become another Birmingham. It became a ghost town within a few years. There is practically nothing left of it, but there is a hiking trail that goes by the site. The trail begins on Farm Road 343 near the intersection of U.S. 69.

Rusk claims to have the longest footbridge in the world. It is 546 feet long. It was built in 1861 and rebuilt in 1889 to enable people to walk back and forth between East and West Rusk in the rainy season. The bridge is on Lone Oak at East 5th Street.

4 *4) This marker near Jacksonville recalls the massacre of 18 white settlers in 1838. 5) A factory in Jacksonville makes most of the cap pistols for the U.S. toy trade.* 5

The first native Texan to become Governor of Texas was born near Rusk. He was James Stephen Hogg and his birthplace has been turned into a state park. It is two miles northeast of Rusk, off U.S. 84. The second native Texan to become Governor came from this county, too. He was Thomas Mitchell Campbell. There is a marker at his birthplace, four miles east of Rusk on the old Rusk-Gallatin Road.

The worst Indian attack in East Texas history occurred in this county. There is a marker at the site seven miles northeast of Jacksonville, on State Highway 175. Eighteen members of the Killough and Williams and Wood families were killed or captured in an attack here in 1838. The families had settled here only a year earlier. They had bought the land in good faith. It happened to be land the Cherokees had been promised in that treaty the Texas Senate refused to ratify.

Another settlement was established in this same area in 1846 and it grew into a town called Larissa. There was a college and the community prospered until shortly after the Civil War. It went into a decline then and it was in ruins by 1885.

A prosperous nurseryman named Wesley Love owned a hill north of Jacksonville. His wife donated the land to the state after Love died in 1925. It is now a roadside park called Love's Lookout. There is a forest fire watch tower on the site, too.

Jacksonville is the biggest, busiest town in the county. There are several factories here. One of them makes most of the cap pistols for the American toy trade. This is the Nichols-

1 *1) This old loom is still in working condition at Forest Hill Plantation near Alto. 2) An Indian city covered the area near this marker at Caddoan Mounds State Park, in prehistoric times.* 2

Kusan plant. It also makes hubs for General Motors steering wheels.

Some accounts of the LaSalle expedition of the 17th century maintain that LaSalle was murdered by his men here in Cherokee County. Most accounts say the murder occurred near Navasota. In the Cherokee County version, LaSalle was buried near the present State Highway 21 close to the present town of Alto.

The early Spanish settlers gave Alto its name because it seemed to be the highest point on the Old Spanish Road. An old log plantation house built here in 1847 is still standing. The plantation is Forest Hills. It is five and one-half miles northwest of Alto on Farm Road 241. The land the old house stands on was granted to James Dill by the government of Mexico in 1828. The house was built in 1847 for Dill's daughter and her husband, Henry Berryman. Mrs. Berryman was Helena Dill. Her family always believed she was the first Anglo child born in Texas. Their records say she was born in Nacogdoches in 1804. It was not until 1821 that Jane Long gave birth at Bolivar to the child other historians have nominated the first Anglo child born in Texas. But Mrs. Dill never got as much press as Mrs. Long did. The Alto Study Club holds open house at the Forest Hills Plantation for several days each fall.

There are some prehistoric Indian mounds four miles southwest of Alto on State Highway 21. The state owns the land. There is a state nursery here, and the State Department of Parks and Wildlife is thinking about developing a park

3

4

3) The Anderson County Courthouse at Palestine was built in 1914. The marker in foreground tells how a Confederate Salt Works, during the Civil War, extracted salt from salt water through a laborious boiling process. The "official" price was $8 per hundred pounds but many people had to pay $20 to buy it. 4) Fort Houston was Anderson County's first headquarters. It was located near Palestine, and there is a marker at the site. The fort was built for protection against Indians. It was abandoned in 1846 after Texas joined the Union.

here that will allow visitors to watch archaeologists digging in the mounds.

Cherokee County might have been an Indian reservation if the Texas Senate had ratified the treaty Sam Houston made with Chief Bowles. The old chief's last home was on the banks of Bowles Creek three miles northwest of Alto. There is a marker, but it is on private property.

ANDERSON COUNTY

Relatives of Cynthia Ann Parker were among the early settlers in what became Anderson County. Cynthia Ann was buried here.

Anderson County was organized in 1846. It was named for K. L. Anderson. He was a native of Tennessee like a lot of other Texas settlers. He came to fight in the revolution and stayed to become a politician and public official. He was the last Vice President of the Republic before Texas became a state.

1

1) The tragic story of Cynthia Ann Parker began near Palestine in the 1830s when settlers from Illinois came to the area that is now Anderson and Limestone counties. Captured as a child, she was adopted by the Comanches and she lived with them most of her life. She could not adjust to her former life when white settlers recaptured her from the Comanches.

Oil is the principal source of income here, but there is substantial farming and ranching, too.

The county seat is the city of Palestine. The present courthouse was built in 1914. The original county seat was Fort Houston. It grew up around a fort established in 1836 by the new government of the Republic. The site was a couple of miles south of the center of the county, and so Palestine was established at the center of the county to serve as the county seat. There is a marker at the original site of Fort Houston, two miles south of town at the intersection of U.S. 79 and Farm Road 1990.

Reverend Daniel Parker gave Palestine its name because the town he lived in in Illinois before he came here was called Palestine. The name is pronounced "Palace-*steen*" and not "stein." Reverend Parker had come to Texas with a party of Primitive Baptists. The party included several other Parkers. Some of the others settled a little farther east in what is now Limestone County. Those Parkers called their settlement Fort Parker, and it was there in May of 1836 that a party of Comanches killed several of the Parkers and kidnapped Cynthia Ann Parker. She was nine years old at the time. The Comanches adopted Cynthia Ann, and she lived with them 25 years. She married Comanche Chief Peta Nocona and they had several children before Cynthia Ann and an infant daughter named Prairie Flower were recaptured in 1860. Cynthia Ann never readjusted to life among the whites. Her baby daughter died in 1864, and Cynthia Ann died shortly afterward. They were buried in a cemetery at the Brush Creek Community near Frankston in what is now Anderson County. Cynthia Ann's son, Quanah Parker, became the last great chief of the Comanches. He caused the settlers farther west a good bit of grief before he was tamed and sent to the reservation in Oklahoma in 1875. The chief visited his mother's grave here in Anderson County in 1910 and paid visits to

2

3

2) This replica of an early Baptist church is on a site used continuously for worship since 1833. It is near Elkhart, and descendants of the Parker family put on a special program about Cynthia Ann each March during the Dogwood Trails Festival. 3) A prominent Confederate Colonel named G. R. Howard, built this home in 1851 and it was occupied by him and his descendants for more than 100 years.

several members of the Parker family before he died in 1911. Quanah is buried near Fort Sill, Oklahoma, and the remains of Cynthia Ann and Prairie Flower have been moved there.

There is a replica of the Pilgrim Baptist Church the Parkers founded here. The site it sits on has been used as a place of worship continuously since 1833, and so this may be the oldest Protestant place of worship in the state. It also may not be. There are other contenders. The location is three miles south of Elkhart on Farm Road 861. Descendants of the Parker family present a special program about Cynthia Ann and the Parkers at this church during the Palestine Dogwood Trails Festival, usually in March.

The oldest house in Palestine is the Howard House at 1011 North Perry Street. It is a museum, and it is open on Saturday and Sunday afternoons exhibiting photographs and furnishings from the earlier days. The house was built in 1851. There

1

2 *1) and 2) show how preservation work has saved a number of fine homes in Anderson County. Top photo shows the elegant H. R. Link House in Palestine. 3) John H. Reagan was Palestine's most famous citizen.* 3

is no admission charge, but donations are encouraged.

Watford Hall is a restored Victorian mansion at 301 S. Magnolia Street. It is furnished with authentic antiques and it is also a museum. There is an admission fee here.

A number of Victorian homes can be seen along South Sycamore, South Magnolia and South Royal Street. These are not normally open to the public.

The park and depot for the Palestine end of the Texas State Railroad is southeast of Palestine on U.S. 84 and well marked. This is the antique steam train described in the chap-

Huge research balloons are launched regularly from a base five miles west of Palestine by the National Center for Atmospheric Research. Launchings can be seen clearly from just outside the base, and launching times can be learned in advance.

1 *1) This location on the Trinity River in Anderson County was where the Magnolia Ferry operated when the Trinity carried steamer traffic. There's at least one old steamboat hull on the bottom here.*

ter on Cherokee County. The phone number for reservations is 214-683-2561.

A statue in Reagan Park near downtown Palestine honors the area's most famous citizen. John H. Reagan had a home just outside Palestine. It was two miles west of town on what is now U.S. 79. There is a marker. (The site is where the original Fort Houston settlement was.) The park and statue are at Crockett Road and Park Avenue in Palestine.

Reagan was a member of the Legislature and a member of Congress. He was Postmaster General in Jefferson Davis' Confederate cabinet. He was a United States Senator after the Civil War, and he left that office in 1891 to serve as the first Chairman of the Texas Railroad Commission. Reagan died in 1905, and the Texas Legislature came to the funeral in a body. Reagan is buried in East Hill Cemetery in Palestine.

The National Center for, Atmospheric Research sends enormous research balloons up periodically from a base five miles west of Palestine on Highway 287. Launching schedules can be obtained from the Palestine Chamber of Commerce 214-729-6066. Visitors are welcome on the base except during launchings. The launchings are plainly visible from outside.

The Palestine Community Forest, west of the city on Highway 287, covers 900 acres. There are three lakes and provisions for swimming, fishing and boating.

2

2) The Bowers Mansion is one of several restored Victorian homes in Palestine. The homes are on South Sycamore, South Magnolia and South Royal streets. They are not usually open to visitors.

The Davy Crockett Dogwood Park on North Link, north of Palestine, has five miles of paved scenic drives, especially scenic during the dogwood season in late March and early April. The Dogwood Trails Festival is usually held in March. Some of the old homes not normally open are open during the festival.

The Engling Wildlife Refuge is 20 miles west of Palestine on Highway 287. It covers more than 10,000 acres. Day campers are welcome, and there is some limited overnight camping. Fishing is allowed. Some limited hunting is allowed sometimes, but don't do any without checking first with the Parks and Wildlife Department. There is no fee here.

The Trinity River runs through Anderson County so there was a riverport here in the early days. It was at Magnolia, 11 miles southwest of Palestine about where Highway 287 and Farm Road 1990 intersect. The last steamer to use the dock here was the *A. S. Ruthven.* She was either dismantled or she fell apart here. The anchor is at the Howard House museum. The hull reappeared in the summer of 1977 when the water in the river dropped below its normal level.

NAVARRO COUNTY

Navarro County has been producing oil longer than any other county in Texas. The oil was first discovered here by crews drilling for water in 1894. The county has been producing oil continuously ever since. The first refinery west of the Mississippi was built here in 1897. Navarro County was producing oil and gas before many people knew what to do with it. Corsicana was the first city in Texas to use natural gas for heating and lighting. The gas for American gas lights was originally made out of coal.

1

1) Jose Antonio Navarro was the Texas patriot who gave his name to Navarro County. He and his uncle were the only two natives of Texas who signed the Texas Declaration of Independence. Navarro suggested the name Corsicana for the county seat here because his father came from Corsica.

Navarro County was organized in 1846. The county was named for Jose Antonio Navarro. He ranks near the top of the list of Texas patriots. Navarro was Spanish, but he sympathized with the Texas colonists from the beginning. He was one of the signers of the Texas Declaration of Independence. He and his uncle, Francisco Ruiz, were the only native Texans among the signers of that document. Navarro fell into the hands of Mexican authorities a few years after the revolution. He was sentenced to death, but he escaped before the sentence was carried out. He was serving in the Legislature when this county was created. They decided to name it for him, and they asked him what name should be given the county seat. He suggested Corsicana because his father came from Corsica. The present courthouse in Corsicana was built in 1905.

Spring Hill may have been the earliest settlement in this county. It was settled in 1838 by Dr. George Washington Hill. He was the first Indian Agent for the Republic of Texas. His settlement was at the western edge of what is now Navarro County, and it went into a decline when the railroad passed it by. What is left is three and a half miles northeast of Dawson, off Farm Road 709. There is a marker at the site of Dr. Hill's trading post, two miles north of Dawson, at the roadside park, on Farm Road 709.

Two widely-known food items originated here in Corsicana. The original recipe for Wolf Brand Chili was put together here in 1895 by a ranch cook and Lyman T. Davis of Corsicana. They started canning their chili in 1921. The company changed hands in 1924 and moved to South Main Street. The new owners expanded production and invented some advertising stunts that spread the fame of Wolf Brand Chili far and wide. Their salesmen traveled around in Model-T Fords with bodies designed to look like the chili can. They carried live wolves in cages on the back. They sold a lot of

2

3

2) The Navarro County Courthouse at Corsicana was built in 1905. 3) This early illustration shows how cabins were built of split logs before the sawmills came. This was the home of Dr. George Washington Hill. He settled in Spring Hill in 1838. The settlement was near Dawson and there is a marker at the site. Spring Hill did not make it as a town because the railroad passed it by after the Civil War.

chili and sold the company to Quaker Oats in 1957.

The Collin Street Bakery has been producing the renowned DeLuxe Fruit Cake for customers all over the world since 1896. The bakery is in a new and modern building at 401 W. 7th Avenue now. Its products are sold only at the bakery or by mail.

The people here were not doing a whole lot with their oil until an outsider named J. S. Cullinan arrived on the scene. That was in 1897. Cullinan was working for Standard Oil, and he was traveling cross country by train on his way to California on Standard Oil business. The train stopped in Corsicana. Cullinan decided to get off and see what he could learn about the oil wells he had heard about. He found out that the oil was being shipped away in railroad tank cars. Cullinan bought some tanks and started buying up the local

1

3

2 *1) The Pioneer Village in Corsicana shows what living conditions were like in Navarro County in frontier days. 2) The spot where this marker stands on Corsicana's Post Office grounds is where the first gas pipeline was located. Corsicana's first oil boom started when city crews drilling for water found crude oil instead. 3) The home Senator James H. Woods built on West Second Street in Corsicana is one of the city's most handsome old buildings. 4) This old photo shows Corsicana's first refinery in action.*

4

5 *5) Corsicana contends that this memorial derrick stands where the Texas oil industry really began. Oil was found here in commercial quantities in the 1890s. 6) At the western end of Navarro County stands the Britton-Dawson House. It was built at Dawson in 1859.* 6

oil. He accumulated 150,000 barrels and then lined up some backing and built a refinery. The refinery operated as J. S. Cullinan and Company and produced kerosene and gasoline. J. S. Cullinan and Company eventually became Magnolia Petroleum (now Mobil). The automobile had not really arrived, and the demand was not great. But Cullinan took the lead in proving that locomotives could burn oil instead of coal. He later founded the Texas Fuel Company at Beaumont to supply oil to railroads. That company became The Texas Company (now Texaco).

The Navarro County Historical Society has done a good job of rounding up antiques and antique buildings in the Pioneer Village. Several authentic very early buildings have been moved here, and the display includes a covered wagon and a stagecoach and many rare old photographs. The Pioneer Village Museum is at 900 West Park Avenue. It is open every weekday, and there is a charge for admission.

Among the historic buildings in Corsicana are:

- The Roger Q. Mills Home at 1200 West 2nd Avenue.
- The Senator James H. Woods Home at 504 West 2nd Avenue.
- The Opera House at 113 South Beaton.

1

1) The Freestone County Courthouse at Fairfield dates back to 1919. The cannon at the right was captured in a Civil War battle in 1862.

FREESTONE COUNTY

Freestone County was organized in 1851. It takes its name from the abundance of rock quarries in the area. Freestone also has some oil and gas, and it also is well supplied with another fuel that is in increasing demand. There are large lignite deposits here. A strip mine supplies fuel for the Big Brown generating plant of the Texas Utilities Company, northeast of Fairfield.

Fairfield is the county seat of Freestone County. The original settlers here about 1849 were planters and they called their settlement Mount Pleasant. They decided to change the name to Fairfield when the county was organized and the community was designated the county seat. Some of the settlers had fond memories of a town named Fairfield in Alabama. There have been a few attempts to move the county government to Teague, but they have not succeeded. The present courthouse was built in 1919. The brass cannon on the lawn is one of several captured from Union forces in Val Verde, New Mexico in 1862.

The Fairfield Female Academy was founded here in 1858, and it flourished until 1889. There is a state marker at the site on East Reunion Street.

The founder of the Moody banking and insurance empire was born in Fairfield in a home his father built in 1860. This is the Moody-Bradley house at 318 Moody Street. It is preserved as a museum. There is a small admission fee. The house is normally open on Sunday afternoons and at other times by appointment with Mrs. Hugh Steward, 214-389-3229.

2

3

2) This is the Moody-Bradley House in Fairfield. 3) W. L. Moody, Sr., built this house for his family in 1860. Moody later moved to Galveston and laid the foundation for the giant banking and insurance empire that made W. L. Moody, Jr. one of the powers of the state in the late 19th and early 20th Centuries. The Moody Foundation is one of the largest private foundations in the U.S.

The old Freestone County Jail is also a museum. It is at 302 East Main Street, and it is maintained by the Freestone County Historical Association. It is open weekdays and Saturdays and on Sunday afternoons. There is a small admission fee. The exhibits include historical artifacts and uniforms from the various military campaigns men from Freestone County have fought in. On the same grounds are two restored pioneer cabins with authentic furnishings.

The Fairfield State Park is on the shores of the lake Texas Utilities Company built to keep its Big Brown generating works cool. The park is six miles northeast of Fairfield off Farm Road 1124. The lake covers 2,400 acres. The park covers 1,400 acres. There are provisions for boating, swimming, fishing, picnicking and camping. The park has 100 camp sites plus some private camping areas. This is a Class I Park with the usual admission fee of $1.00 per vehicle unless you have the annual permit or passport. Reservations can be

1

1) This restored log cabin and 2) the former Freestone County Jail are parts of the museum maintained by the Freestone County Historical Association. It is on East Main Street in Fairfield. Exhibits include uniforms local men wore in various wars and military campaigns.

2

made by writing to the Park Supervisor, Route 2, Box 269, Fairfield 75840 or by calling 214-389-4514.

One of the major towns in Freestone County in earlier times was Steward's Mill. It had the usual grist mill and a sawmill and a cotton gin. It was a busy place. Dr. James Bonner and Jeremiah Stewart built a general store here in 1867 and the place is still standing. Frank Bragg still sells livestock feed and soft drinks here. There is very little other merchandise but a lot of memories. There are old ledgers here going back to the days when $2.00 bought 6 pounds of coffee. Steward's Mill is about 10 miles north of Fairfield where Farm Road 833 and Farm Road 2547 meet.

One of the great early Negro blues singers was born and raised in this area. There is some question about exactly where Blind Lemon Jefferson was born. But he is buried in the Wortham Negro Cemetery at Wortham at the western edge of Freestone County.

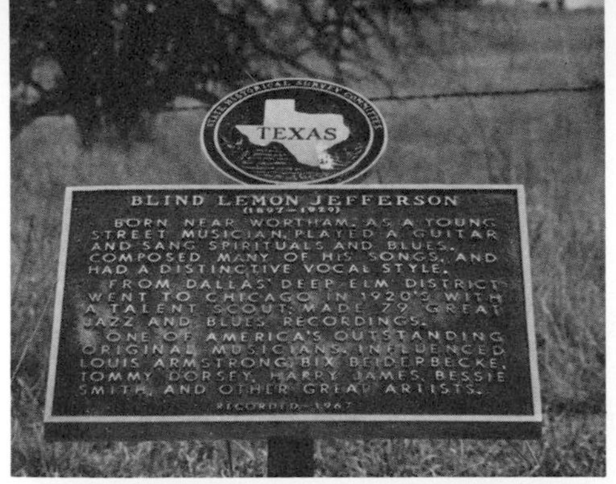

3

3) This plaque honors Blind Lemon Jefferson. He was an early day blues singer who had a major influence on the popular music of the 1930s and 1940s. 4) Bragg's Store at Steward's Mill was built in 1867 and it is still open for business, but barely.

4

Interstate 45 passes close by Fairfield and it misses Teague, so Fairfield probably will grow faster than Teague over the near future. But Teague upstaged Fairfield during the railroad era because Teague had a larger place in the railroad scheme of things. The Trinity and Brazos Valley Railroad had its machine shops in Teague. Teague became a stopping point for the glamorous and now extinct Sam Houston Zephyr streamliner when the Burlington-Rock Island bought out the Trinity and Brazos Valley. The old Teague Passenger Depot is now a railroad museum featuring a number of relics from the glory days of railroading. The museum is open most of the day Saturday and on Sunday afternoons. They re-live the pioneer days here in Teague every summer with a Western Days celebration, usually around the Fourth of July. Somebody always recalls then that the Trinity and Brazos Valley Railroad was better known in the early 1900's as the Boll Weevil Line. This was because so many of the line's passengers in those days were farmers and agricultural experts traveling to conferences on what to do about the damage the detested boll weevils were doing to the cotton crops.

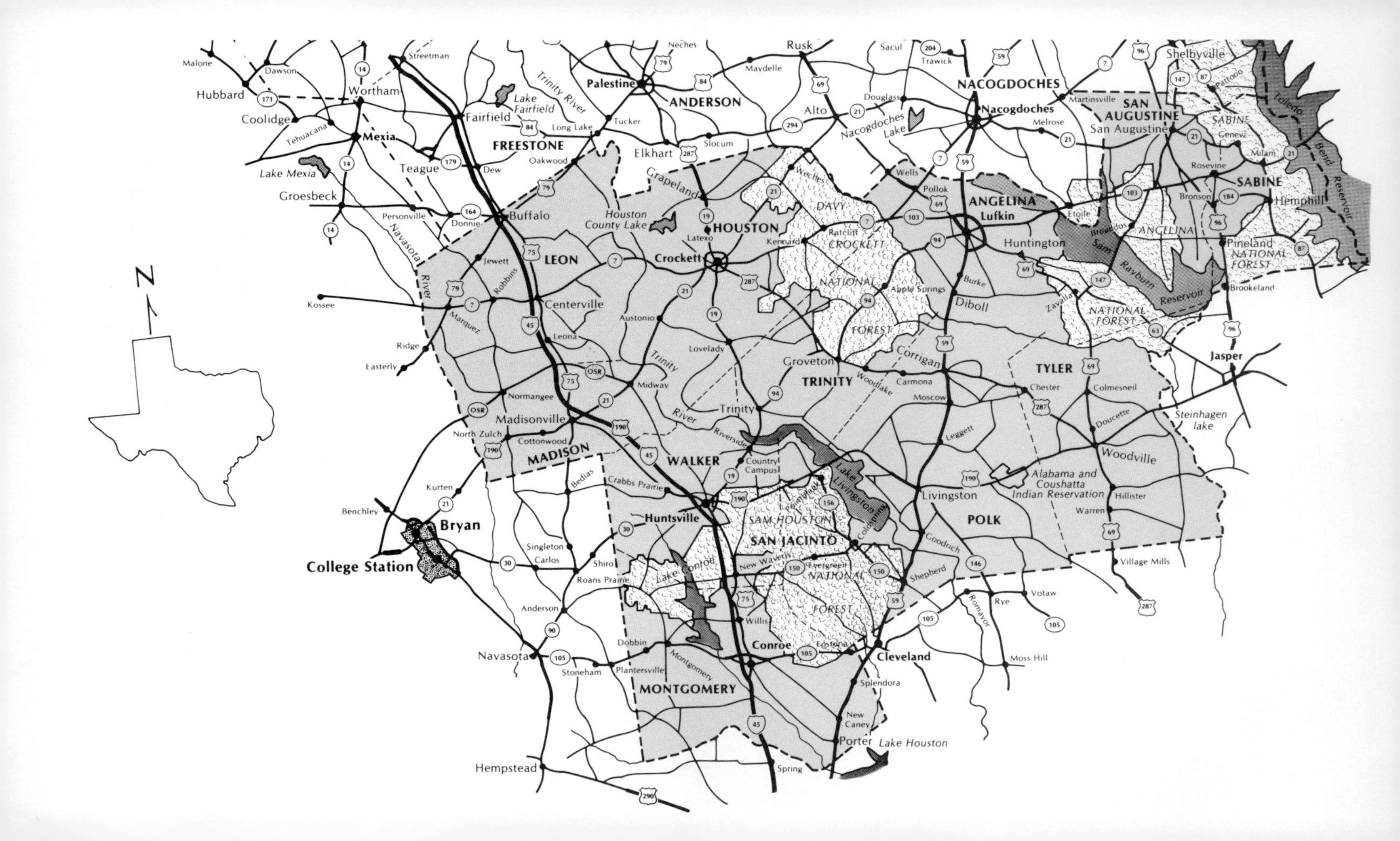

N
NACOGDOCHES
Nacogdoches
SAN AUGUSTINE
San Augustine
SABINE
Hemphill
Toledo Bend Reservoir
ANGELINA
Lufkin
Huntington
Sam Rayburn Reservoir
ANGELINA NATIONAL FOREST
SABINE NATIONAL FOREST
ANDERSON
Palestine
FREESTONE
Fairfield
Lake Fairfield
Trinity River
HOUSTON
Crockett
Houston County Lake
Grapeland
DAVY CROCKETT NATIONAL FOREST
LEON
Centerville
Buffalo
Jewett
TRINITY
Groveton
Trinity
TYLER
Woodville
Jasper
Steinhagen lake
Alabama and Coushatta Indian Reservation
POLK
Livingston
Lake Livingston
WALKER
Huntsville
SAM HOUSTON NATIONAL FOREST
SAN JACINTO
MADISON
Madisonville
Bryan
College Station
Navasota
MONTGOMERY
Conroe
Lake Conroe
Cleveland
Lake Houston
Hempstead
Mexia
Teague
Wortham
Groesbeck
Lake Mexia
Hubbard
Coolidge
Navasota River
Rusk
Alto
Nacogdoches Lake
Diboll
Corrigan
Kossee

The Forests and Lakes

Montgomery, San Jacinto, Walker, Trinity
Madison, Leon, Houston, Angelina, San Augustine,
Sabine, Tyler and Polk Counties

Everybody everywhere has heard something about Texas. Anybody coming here for the first time from anywhere else has some idea of what Texas is. The ideas are often wrong and always incomplete.

The thing newcomers seem to come here least expecting to find is the timber. Texas has been cutting and shipping timber for more than 75 years. But visitors more often than not are surprised to find most of the eastern section of the state covered with pine forests. The pines were here long before the white man came. They might be all gone now if it hadn't been for William Goodrich Jones. He was a banker in Galveston and Temple. But Jones liked trees better than banking. East Texas historian Bob Bowman credits Jones with being the first to realize that the East Texas Forest could be a continuing resource. Anyway, he was the first to do something about it. The early logging and lumber companies cut down everything in sight and then moved on to another location to do the same thing again. Jones got upset about this in the 1880's and started a personal campaign for conservation and replanting. He pushed the Legislature into establishing a Department of Forestry, and he helped get the National Forests established. Texas now has four National Forests and four State Forests. One of the State Forests is named for the

1

1) If you think Conroe in Montgomery County is a busy place today, you should have been here when this photo was taken during the 1930s oil boom. Traffic jams and swarms of leasehounds came as a new experience for what had been a quiet little piney woods town.

father of Texas forest conservation. The William Goodrich Jones State Forest is outside Conroe, in Montgomery County. Jones died in 1950. His personal files and records are in the library at Stephen F. Austin State University in Nacogdoches.

There are forests and lakes all over East Texas. But the big lakes and all the National Forests and two of the State Forests are concentrated in this part of the state. I-45 runs along the western edge of this section of the state. But old U.S. 75 does, too, all the way from Conroe to beyond Fairfield. Use U.S. 75 unless you particularly enjoy being passed by trucks.

MONTGOMERY COUNTY

Montgomery County is growing about as fast as any comparable area in the country. Part of the reason is the county's proximity to Houston. But Montgomery County has plenty of resources of its own.

Montgomery County is rich in oil and gas and timber. Many people live and work here. Many others commute from homes here to jobs in Houston. They are trading commuting time for lower taxes and a more relaxed lifestyle. Commuter villages are growing up among the resort developments around Lake Conroe.

Montgomery County was organized in 1837. It was named for U.S. General Richard Montgomery. The county seat is Conroe. This city began as a little settlement living off Isaac Conroe's sawmill. The settlement grew as the timber industry grew. It started to decline when the timber began to play out. But George Strake discovered oil and gas a few miles outside town in the early 1930's, and Conroe has been booming ever since.

2

3 *2) and 3) show how some developers in Montgomery County have integrated their construction into the piney woods to preserve much of the natural beuuty. 4) Lakeside condominiums are attracting year-round residents.* 4

Conroe has been the county seat since 1889. Before that, the county government was based in Montgomery and in Willis.

Montgomery is the original town in Montgomery County. Montgomery was settled about the time of the Texas Revolution. Montgomery is situated where State Highway 105 intersects State Highway 149 west of Lake Conroe. Some of the early buildings are still here and some of them are open each spring during the annual Montgomery Trek. Sam Houston often visited Montgomery, and he sometimes stayed at the Peter Willis home at College Street and Eugenia. This house was built in 1854. It is called "Magnolia." They say it was named for the same woman the Magnolia Petroleum Company was named for. "Magnolia" is now the home of the R. T. Weisingers.

Montgomery County is popular with antique collectors. The back roads in the county pass by some fairly fancy

1

2

3 *1) The First State Bank is the oldest commercial building in Montgomery. 2) This is the Montgomery County Courthouse. 3) In October Magnolia hosts the Renaissance Festival.*

antique shops and some very plain ones, too. One of the plainest is Mrs. Winslow's on Highway 105 on the edge of Montgomery. Some dealers buy old things and fix them up for sale. Mrs. Winslow lets her customers have the fun of fixing up. She sells it the way she finds it, but not cheaply. A lot of what she has for sale looks like junk. She has a sign outside inviting you to ask the price if you think it is junk.

Magnolia is the site of the Texas Renaissance Festival. The festival happens every weekend in October on a site on Farm Road 1774 northwest of town. People gather here to eat and drink and make merry the way they imagine people did in England in medieval times.

4

5

4) Two warring factions of residents here supposedly inspired this community's unique name. 5) The Peter Willis House in Montgomery was built in 1854 and Sam Houston occasionally visited here during his trips through the area.

The town of Willis on U.S. 75 north of Conroe was once a tobacco center. There were several cigar factories here in the late 1890's. But it has been years now since any tobacco was grown here.

The most picturesquely named settlement in Montgomery is "Cut 'N Shoot." It supposedly was named this after they had a fracas here over the design of the steeple for a new church building. It is not just a nickname. There is a post office at Cut 'N Shoot.

There are marinas and boat ramps open to the public around Lake Conroe, off State Highway 105 and Farm Road 1907 west of Interstate 45.

1 *From the west shore in midwinter, Lake Livingston looks cold and forbidding. But it draws fishing and water sports enthusiasts the year around.*

There are provisions for hiking, swimming, picnicking and fishing in the W. G. Jones State Forest. The forest is off Farm Road 1488 west of Interstate 45. No hunting is allowed in the state forests. License requirements for fishing are the same in the State and National Forests as they are anywhere else in the state. People under 17 and over 65 fish free. The sports fishing license fee for residents over 17 and under 65 is $4.50 a year, and the license period is September 1 through August 31. Non-residents pay $10.50 for a fishing license, regardless of age. But temporary licenses are available to non-residents for less. The licenses can be obtained at almost any sporting goods store or bait camp.

SAN JACINTO COUNTY

The Sam Houston National Forest covers part of Montgomery County and part of Walker County. It covers most of San Jacinto County.

2

3

2) This is the Big Creek Scenic Area eight miles south of Coldspring in San Jacinto County. A national forest covers much of the county attracting nature lovers and hikers. 3) San Jacinto County's courthouse at Coldspring was built in 1918. It contains a small museum.

This area was settled early because the Trinity River flows through it, and the Trinity was the original commercial artery in this part of the state. But no major town ever developed in the county. The only major highway today is U.S. 59. It passes through only the southeast corner of the county and misses the county seat.

San Jacinto County was organized in 1870. It was named for the battle. The county seat is Coldspring. The population of Coldspring is under 1,000. The present courthouse was built in 1918 after an earlier model at another site burned in 1915. There is a small museum in the courthouse. It is open daily and free.

There is some oil and gas, some farming and a lot of lumbering in San Jacinto County. Recreation has become a major industry here since Lake Livingston has been completed. The

1

1) San Jacinto County's old county jail was built in the 1880s. It was equipped with a hangman's trap so that executions could be carried out here. It was never used.

northeastern corner of the county fronts on the lake. There are several marinas and campgrounds and some plush resorts along State Highway 156 north of Coldspring.

Sam Houston once had a country home he called Raven Hill near the present town of Oakhurst on U.S. 190. There is only a marker at the site now. It is three miles southeast of Oakhurst, about two miles off Farm Road 946. The Cherokees called Houston "The Raven." He was proud of it. A Cherokee chief gave him the name when he adopted him. That was before Houston came to Texas.

The second Governor of Texas had a large plantation in what is now San Jacinto County. George T. Wood came to Texas from Georgia in 1839. He brought his family and 30 slaves, and he established himself on the west bank of the Trinity. The site was part of Liberty County at the time. Wood was elected to the State Senate after Texas joined the Union. He resigned to join the Army when the war between the United States and Mexico began. Wood fought with some distinction and there was considerable controversy for years afterward over whether he or J. Pinckney Henderson had the most to do with winning the Battle of Monterrey. Henderson had taken leave of absence from the Governor's Office to fight in the war. The controversy did Wood no political harm apparently. Henderson chose not to run for another term as Governor after the war ended, and Wood was elected to succeed him in 1847.

Wood died at his plantation home in 1858, and he was buried here in an unmarked grave. The state put up a monu-

2

Both of these San Jacinto County structures carry the state's historic medallion. 2) This is the Coldspring United Methodist Church and 3) J. M. Hansboro's law office on the town square in Coldspring.

3

ment at the site of the plantation in 1936 during the centennial when so many historical sites were being marked. But somebody made a mistake in 1936, and the official state marker near the present town of Point Blank refers to the second Governor of Texas as George Thomas Wood. His name actually was George Tyler Wood. Wood introduced the bill that created Tyler County while he was serving in the Senate in 1846. The Tyler County seat of Woodville was named in his honor.

Almost any drive on any road in San Jacinto County is a scenic drive, but the Forest Service has designated a Big Creek Scenic Area south of Coldspring. The Big Creek Scenic Area is about eight miles south of town, off State Highway 150 on Forest Service Road 217.

The Double Lake Recreation Area in the Sam Houston National Forest on Farm Road 2025, four miles south of Coldspring, has provisions for camping and picnicking and swimming. There are shelters and hiking trails, and there is a fee.

There is a hiking trail extending the length of the Sam

1 *1) The Walker County Courthouse was built in 1970, replacing one built in 1889. The architectural style suggests the old Plantation, double-balcony look that characterized much 19th Century home building in the Southwest.*

Houston National Forest. It is called the Lone Star Trail. It is marked with white aluminum markers. It passes through two camping areas. And primitive camping is permitted anywhere along the trail the year around.

A retired couple named Hill established a herb farm off the road between Cleveland and Conroe (State Highway 105) in the southwestern tip of this county several years ago. The Hilltop Herb Farm has since become famous all over the country. The Hills now grow all kinds of herbs. They can and sell a variety of specialty items and they serve meals at the farm. You can visit without a reservation, but don't expect to eat without one. The phone number is 713-592-5859.

WALKER COUNTY

Walker County shares Lake Livingston and the Sam Houston National Forest with San Jacinto County. There is a similarity of scenery, but Walker County is a much busier place.

This county was established in 1846. It was named originally for U.S. Treasury Secretary R. J. Walker. Then the residents decided they wanted their county named for a Texas Ranger instead. They didn't have to change the name. The Ranger they wanted to honor was named S. H. Walker. It is still Walker County.

The county seat is Huntsville. The town was founded as an Indian Trading Post in 1836. Sam Houston lived here and died here and commuters from the city they named for Sam are beginning to move in.

The courthouse at Huntsville is a relatively new one. It was built in 1970 after the courthouse built in 1889 burned down.

Much of the southern part of Walker County is in the Sam

2) Huntsville State Park is just south of Huntsville. It has provisions for swimming, fishing, boating and camping. 2

Houston National Forest. Lake Livingston is at the northeastern corner of the county. Lake Conroe reaches into the southwestern corner, and there is a major state park in the county.

The main highway between Dallas and Houston passed along the west side of the courthouse square here for many years. But now the interstate passes clear of the downtown area as it does every other downtown area between Houston and Dallas. The loss of the heavy through traffic has not had any noticeably depressing effect upon downtown Huntsville. The town is growing steadily. There is some oil and gas here, but ranching and farming and operating the prison system and the Sam Houston State University provide most of the income.

Sam Houston State University began as the Sam Houston Normal Institute in 1879. It was also known as the Sam Houston State Teachers' College for a time before it became a University.

Several schools were established in Huntsville before 1879. Austin College was founded by the Presbyterian Church in 1849. Sam Houston was one of the original members of the board. Austin College was moved to Sherman in the 1870's. But the original Austin Hall still stands on what is now the campus of Sam Houston State University.

1

1) Sam Houston State University was founded in Huntsville nearly a century ago. It has grown to university status since World War II. This is Austin Hall, near downtown Huntsville.

The Congress of the Republic of Texas started worrying about what to do with lawbreakers in 1842. The first decision to establish a state penitentiary was made then. But the lawmakers failed to appropriate enough money to carry out what they ordered. The first prison was not built until 1849. The state has tried all kinds of ways from the beginning to make the prison system pay its own way. A cloth mill was established in the prison in 1854. This mill stayed very busy during the Civil War turning out cloth for the Confererate Army.

The state also experimented with a furnace and foundry at Rusk and even leased out the entire system to private operators for a period of about 30 years in the late 1800's. The prison system began buying farms in 1885, and it now operates large farms in Walker County and several other counties.

The main prison unit is called "The Walls." It is just north of the square in downtown Huntsville. Tours can sometimes be arranged for organized groups, with plenty of advance notice. There are no regular tours. But the annual Texas Prison Rodeo draws good crowds to the prison arena adjacent to the The Walls every Sunday in October. And the prisoners' craft shop is open 8:00 a.m. to 5:00 p.m. daily except Mondays and Tuesdays selling articles made by the prisoners.

The Sam Houston Park in the 1800 block of Avenue L includes a museum displaying many of the personal possessions of the first president and principal hero of the Republic of Texas. The park is across from the Sam Houston University campus near downtown. Two of General Houston's homes and his law office and a carriage house are in the park.

Few men in history have won more honors or held more offices than Sam Houston. He was born in Virginia. He moved to Tennessee as a young man, and there he first made friends with the Cherokee Indians. Houston served in the U.S. Army and then went into politics in Tennessee. He was elected to Congress and then he was elected Governor of Tennessee. He

2 *2) The Texas Prison Rodeo draws large crowds to "the Walls" where inmates stage one of the wildest rodeos seen in Texas. This contestant is "up" in the saddle bronc riding. The rodeo is staged every Sunday in October.*

married the daughter of a prominent citizen, but it apparently was an unhappy arrangement. Mrs. Houston left him and Houston resigned the Governor's office and left Tennessee. He took up with the Cherokees again. They had moved west to Arkansas and Oklahoma. Houston lived with them and helped them manage their affairs and took a Cherokee wife. He apparently had some kind of commission from the President to work with the Cherokees, and he was ostensibly on business for the Cherokees when he first came to Texas in 1832. He quickly got caught up in the maneuvering that led up to the Revolution, and he was listed as a resident of Nacogdoches by 1833.

Houston was a delegate to the Convention of 1836 at Washington-on-the-Brazos. He signed the Declaration of Independence there and was named Commander in Chief of the Texas Army two days later. Travis lost the Alamo to Santa Anna a short time later and Houston disappointed a lot of Texans by leading his little Army in a general retreat toward Louisiana. He salvaged the situation and his reputation at San Jacinto on April 21, 1836.

Houston was elected President of the Republic in 1836 and again in 1841. He was elected to the U.S. Senate as soon as Texas joined the Union. He was a senator when he bought the home he called Woodland at the site that is now Sam Houston

1

1) Sam Houston had a large reputation as politician and soldier before he ever came to Texas. He won additional fame here as head of the Texas revolutionary army and founder of a new republic that later became a state. 2) This is the Sam Houston Memorial Museum in Huntsville.

2

Park. Houston was not in sympathy with the Southern secession sentiment. But he was elected Governor, anyway, when he left the Senate in 1859. Texans decided to secede. Governor Houston took the position that the decision made Texas a Republic again and not a part of the Confederacy. He refused to take an oath of allegiance to the Confederacy. The Legislature removed him from office and moved Lieutenant Governor Edward Clark up to take his place. Houston had been forced to sell his home in Huntsville and Raven Hill, too, to pay off some of his political debts. He retired to a rented house on the outskirts of Huntsville. This was the place known as "The Steamboat House." The house had been built by President Rufus Bailey of Austin College. Houston died in the Steamboat House in 1863 at the age of 70. He was survived by Margaret Lea Houston and eight children. Houston had married Margaret Lea in 1840 between terms as President of Texas. She was a staunch Baptist. She persuaded him to be

3

4

Here are two of the homes that Sam Houston occupied. 3) This is the Steamboat House where Houston died at the age of 70. 4) The Woodland was one of his favorite earlier homes.

baptized into her church in 1845, and it is said that his drinking attracted considerably less attention after that.

Jack Josey of Houston bought the Steamboat House in 1936 and gave it to the state to be moved to the Sam Houston Park where it is today.

Sam Houston is buried in Oakwood Cemetery a few blocks from the park where his homes are.

The Huntsville State Park west of Interstate 45 and south of Huntsville in the Sam Houston National Forest is one of the state's Class I parks. There are provisions for camping and fishing, swimming and boating. There are trailer connec-

1

1) This is the Trinity County Courthouse at Groveton. The county had two earlier county seats before settling at Groveton in 1882. This building went up in 1914. Trinity was settled early in the 19th Century like many other East Texas counties because of its location on the navigable Trinity River.

tions and shelters for rent. There is an admission fee of $1.00 per vehicle unless you have an annual permit or parklands' passport. The phone number for reservations at the Huntsville State Park is 713-295-5644. If you have other questions about the parks or hunting or fishing, the State Department of Parks and Wildlife now has a toll free information number. The number is 1-800-252-9327.

The Stubblefield Lake Recreation Area in the Sam Houston National Forest has shelters and provisions for camping and picnicking and hiking. There is a fee. The Stubblefield Lake Recreation Area is 12 miles north and west of New Waverly by way of Farm Road 1375 and Forest Service Road 208.

TRINITY COUNTY

Trinity County is another one of those counties without a major city or a major highway.

The county is bounded on the southwest by the Trinity River and Lake Livingston and on the northeast by the Neches River. More than one third of the county is in the Davy Crockett National Forest.

There is limited oil and gas production here. But the county lives mostly from farming, ranching and the lumber business.

This is another one of those counties that was settled early because it had frontage on the Trinity River. There was an important river port, in the southeastern corner of the county, called Sebastopol. There is a community in the area now, because it is on the shores of Lake Livingston. But there is nothing left of the old port of Sebastopol except a granite marker on Farm Road 356 a few miles southeast of Trinity. Some vandal somewhere must have a substantial collection of bronze stars. The star is missing from this marker and stars are missing from similar markers all over the state.

2) Trinity is the larget town in Trinity County. During the boom days of the lumber business, it was even more of a timber center than it is now. But a lot of pulp wood is still cut in this area. 2

The National Register of Historic Places lists an historic house in Trinity. The Register says the Ranald McDonald House at Maple and San Jacinto is the only remaining 19th century house in Trinity with any architectural significance. If that was so, there are no such houses in Trinity now. There was a group in Trinity trying to preserve the McDonald house and another group wanted to tear it down. The preservation group got the house listed in the National Register to prevent it from being torn down. But the National Register cannot prevent old buildings from burning. The Ranald McDonald house stood for nearly 100 years. But it burned after it was added to the National Register of Historic Places.

The county seat of Trinity County is Groveton. The town was founded by the IGN Railroad in 1881 and it became the county seat in 1882. The Trinity and Sabine Timber Company had a big mill here from the 1880's until the late 1930's. The present courthouse in Groveton was built in 1914. It is handsome and well kept.

The Trinity County seat was in three other communities before it was established in Groveton. Sumpter was designated the county seat when the county was established. The county government moved to Trinity in 1873 after a fire destroyed the courthouse in Sumpter. The government moved to Pennington in 1874 and stayed there until it moved to Groveton in 1882.

1 *Only granite markers show where these substantial Trinity County towns were located in the 19th Century. 1) Sebastopol was an important river shipping point of the 1850s. It died when the railroads replaced the river boats. 2) Sumpter once was the county seat and it dwindled away after the county government was removed to Trinity.* 2

Pennington and Trinity both survived the loss of the county government headquarters. Trinity is the biggest town in the county today. But Sumpter died after the government moved away. Sumpter was just north of U.S. Highway 287, about five and one-half miles east of Groveton. There is a granite marker at the site. It is on private property. There is no sign of a building or a foundation or even a chimney. But the old Sumpter Cemetery is nearby. Markers in the cemetery go back to the 1830's, so there apparently was a settlement at Sumpter before the county was organized.

Sumpter was the home of Texas' most notorious gunman and killer. John Wesley Hardin was the son of a Methodist preacher and lawyer. He was born in 1853 and he was shot to death by a constable in El Paso in 1895. Hardin killed a man when he was fifteen. He killed six more by the time he was seventeen. He had killed more than thirty men by the time he died. Hardin was not an ordinary hoodlum. He was handsome and gentlemanly, and he seemed able to convince himself that all those killings were unavoidable and necessary.

The Kickapoo Picnic Area in the Davy Crockett National Forest is three miles east of Groveton on U.S. 287. It is not elaborate. There is no overnight camping, but there are hiking trails and provisions for picnicking and day camping.

Hunting is allowed in the National Forests in Texas, but it is subject to state regulations. All non-residents must have licenses to hunt in Texas. All residents must have licenses if they hunt outside their home counties or hunt deer or turkeys. Hunting licenses can be obtained at most sporting goods stores and tackle shops. The fee for residents is $5.25 but resi-

3

3) John Wesley Hardin was not your run of the mill outlaw. He came from an upright family in Trinity County and tried repeatedly during his life to lead a normal family life. He became a lawyer but he kept getting into various scrapes with the law and with adversaries until the day he was shot in the back in 1895. He was handsome and well-mannered, but authorities consider him the most dangerous gunman ever to operate in Texas.

dents uner 17 and over 65 can get exempt licenses for $1.25. The Department of Parks and Wildlife has two free pamphlets available. They are "Texas Hunting Guide" and "Texas Fishing Guide." You can get them by writing to the Texas Department of Parks and Wildlife, John H. Reagan Building, Austin 78701. There is also a "Hunter's Guide to Texas" available from Post Office Box 12013, Austin 78711 for $4.35 a copy. The price includes postage and tax. This book has information on where various kinds of game can be found, including the names of property owners and the prices they charge for hunting on their property. Most hunting in Texas is done on private property by arrangement with the owner.

MADISON COUNTY

Madison County is on the Old San Antonio Road, and the LaBahia Road also passed through here. Interstate 45 passes right through the center of the county. But it remains a relatively quiet place. There is some oil and gas, but farming and ranching are the chief occupations. The farms include a very big mushroom farm.

The Old San Antonio Road from San Antonio to the Louisiana border and the LaBahia Road from Goliad to the lower Louisiana border followed the same route west of the Trinity River. They split at the Trinity. The Old San Antonio Road headed northeastward. LaBahia headed southeastward. Both trails used the same crossing on the Trinity. The crossing was five miles east of the present town of Midway. Joel Leakey established a ferry service here in 1821. Nathaniel

1 *1) Here is where the old Robbins-Clapp Ferry operated from about 1821 until 1930 when the modern bridge was built across the Trinity River in Madison County. Only a small boat ramp marks the spot today. 2) The owners of this establishment in Madisonville created a sort of artificial cave to match Mother Nature's ideal growing conditions for mushrooms.*

2

Robbins bought the ferry in the 1830's and he operated it until the 1850's. It was known as Robbins ferry for a long time after Elisha Clapp bought it. Descendants of Elisha Clapp operated the ferry at the historic river crossing for almost 80 years until the Clapp's Ferry bridge was built in 1930. There is a little boat ramp at the site today.

The county seat of Madison County is Madisonville. The county and the town were named for President Madison. The present courthouse was finished in 1969. An earlier courthouse burned in 1968 after serving the county for a hundred years.

3

1) The Madison County Courthouse in Madisonville was completed in 1969. The marker (foreground) is a memorial to the county's Civil War confederate veterans. 2) Madisonville has a "Yesteryear" Museum just north of town that recalls what some local buildings looked like in the county's past.

4

The big event in Madisonville is the annual celebration of the Sidewalk Cattlemen's Association in June.

The Yesteryear Museum on the Old San Antonio Road north of Madisonville and just west of I-45 and U.S. 75 is a collection of antique furniture and equipment and implements. The collection is housed in several buildings. Some of the buildings are authentic relics and some are replicas. There is a blacksmith shop and a saloon. The operator keeps a buffalo on the premises for added atmosphere. There is an admission charge of $1.00 for adults and 50c for children.

The Old Spanish Road forms the boundary between Madi-

1

2

3

1) A pot-bellied stove of long ago can still be fired up at the Yesteryear Museum near Madisonville. 2) Here stood Trinidad before its demise a century ago. 3) The marker indicates that the King's Highway, or Old Spanish Road passed by this location.

son County and Leon County. State Highway 21 follows the route of the Old San Antonio Road for most of the distance between San Antonio and the Louisiana Line. But 21 and the OSR take slightly different routes through here. State Highway 21 combines with U.S. 190 between Madisonville and Bryan somewhat to the south of the original OSR. Normangee sits astride the OSR, northwest of Madisonville. Part of the town is in Madison County and part is in Leon County. Here in Normangee and all along the way, the original route of the Old San Antonio Road is marked with slabs of granite installed by the Daughters of the American Revolution.

The original San Antonio Road was close to being forgotten about until the Legislature decided in 1912 that it ought to be preserved. The Legislature appropriated money to pay for a survey. W. N. Zivley got the job. He marked off the route and the Legislature directed the Highway Department to establish and maintain a State Highway along it. Highway 21 is the result. Zivley had some help from the mesquite trees.

4

4) The Leon County Courthouse at Centerville was built in 1886. The county government moved to Centerville in 1851 to be nearer the center of the county. This was more important in the horse and buggy days than it is today.

Mesquite trees are not native to this part of the state. But they are growing along the route of the OSR. The early Spaniards carried mesquite beans to feed to their animals when they traveled. They and the animals dropped beans along the way and trees sprouted, so Zivley knew where the mesquite trees were the trail probably was.

LEON COUNTY

Leon County was organized in 1844. It was named for Spanish settler Martin de Leon. He was the founder of the city of Victoria.

The county has a little oil and gas; ranching and farming produce most of the income here.

The county seat of Leon County is Centerville on U.S. 75 at State Highway 7. The original county seat was the town of Leona.

John Durst is buried in the old Durst family cemetery two miles outside Leona, off Farm Road 977. Durst was a kind of Texas Paul Revere. He was a member of the Legislature of the Mexican State of Coahuila and Texas at Monclova back in 1836. He got early word of Santa Anna's plan to march into Texas to put down the Revolution. Durst rode his horse all the way from Monclova to Nacogdoches to spread the word.

The government of Leon County was moved to Centerville in 1851 because this is the center of the county. This was a lot more important in the horse and buggy days than it is today.

The first brick courthouse here was built in 1858. It burned in 1885 and was rebuilt in 1886. This is the courthouse still in use today. Centerville is one of our smaller county seats. There are fewer than 1,000 people here.

The area that is now Leon County was part of the land the Mexican government granted to Stephen F. Austin and

1

2

1) Some courthouses preserve with pride the elegant old stairs and bannisters within the buildings. This is the interior stairway of the Leon County Courthouse. 2) The old Lyon Hotel in Buffalo dates back to the time when the IGN Railroad brought lots of passengers and salesmen through Buffalo. 3) Nothing remains of Old Fort Boggy near Centerville except a rotting sign.

3

4

4) The movies and television made the name of Davy Crockett so famous that it is now difficult to separate man and myth. The town of Crockett is named for him but he did not live here. He only camped here on his way to die at the Alamo.

Samuel May Williams for colonizing. The early settlements were along the Trinity River. There were riverboat landings and small towns at Cairo and Commerce and Brookfield's Bluff. All of them have vanished.

A company of Minute Men established a fort here in 1841 during the days of the Republic. It was called Fort Boggy, and it was about five and one-half miles south of Centerville off U.S. 75. The site is on private property.

The biggest town in Leon County is Buffalo on U.S. 75 at the northern edge of the county. Buffalo grew up after the I.G.N. Railroad came through. Several of the early Negro country blues musicians got their start in Buffalo. The Buffalo Association has a campground outside town. Negro Baptists still gather here for meetings occasionally. But the meetings do not attract the crowds they did in the days before television. In the early 1900's the meetings on the Buffalo Association campground sometimes drew 2,000 people. They camped here and ate barbecue and fried fish and listened to preachers and musicians. It is said that Lightnin' Hopkins, Mance Lipscomb and Blind Lemon Jefferson all found here the encouragement that sent them on to bigger things.

HOUSTON COUNTY

Houston County was organized in 1837. It was named for General Houston and the county seat was named for Alamo hero Davy Crockett.

The county has some oil and gas income, but farms and ranches are the biggest money makers here. Lignite was discovered here in 1904.

1

1) The Old San Antonio Road generally follows State Highway 21 from San Antonio to the Louisiana border. Here, it winds through Houston County. Many of the pioneers and adventurers who turned Texas into a republic and then a state came in by this route. 2) Houston County's courthouse at Crockett was built in 1937. 3) Every year for a long time the old fiddlers have gotten together in Crockett for their June festival. Here are two of the real old-timers photographed in 1949.

2

3

4

5

6

4) An early stage coach stop developed here from a log cabin built by Joseph D. Rice. (See photo on the next page) 5) A soaring example of Victorian architecture is the Aldrich House in Crockett. 6) This is the Monroe Crook House in Crockett.

Davy Crockett is supposed to have camped overnight here on his way to the Alamo. The reputed campsite is marked with a plaque. It is at the underpass where State Highway 7 and State Highway 21 intersect. The town was named for Crockett after his friend, A. E. Gossett, donated the town site.

The original courthouse here was a log fort. It burned in 1865, and most of the county records burned with it. The present courthouse was built in 1937. Crockett has a Fiddlers' Festival every June and a rodeo every July.

Crockett is on the Old San Antonio Road, so it has been an important stopping point for 140 years. Some of the early buildings burned with the courthouse in 1865. But the city has a number of old buildings and old homes.

Some of the homes with historical markers are the Monroe

1 *1) This is the log cabin that Joseph Rice developed into an inn in the 1840s. It has been restored and moved to the Mission Tejas State Park at Weches in the Davy Crockett National Forest. 2) In the same state park is this building — a replica of the old Spanish Mission San Francisco de los Tejas. It originally was established in 1690.*

2

Crook House at 707 E. Houston, built by a nephew of President James Monroe; the A. T. Monroe House at 402 S. 7th, now a funeral home; and the A. A. Aldrich House at 206 N. 7th.

The home of early settler A. E. Gossett is outside town. It is one and a half miles east on State Highway 21.

There is a state marker five miles east of Crockett on State Highway 21 where Joseph R. Rice built a small house in 1828. Rice abandoned the place shortly afterward because he was worried about the Indians. He returned in 1830 and later expanded his log cabin into an inn. The site has remained in the Rice family ever since. But the family of Joseph Rice's grandson donated the old log inn building to the state. It has been moved to the Mission Tejas State Park at Weches on State Highway 21 in the Davy Crockett National Forest, and it has been restored to something like the condition it probably was in during the 1840's and 50's. It is not a replica. It is the restored original.

3

4

3) Ratcliff Lake Recreation Area is one of two recreational areas in that portion of the Davy Crockett National Forest that lies within Houston County. The other is Neches Bluff, off Highway 21. 4) This marker is near a former settlement in Houston County called Augusta. The community is gone but the memory of the Indian massacre of the 1830s is preserved by the marker. It is on Farm Road 227, east of Grapeland.

There is also a replica of the old Spanish Mission San Francisco de los Tejas in the Mission Tejas State Park. The original mission was established in 1690 when the Old San Antonio Road was new. The mission was abandoned in 1693 and re-established in 1716 for a time. The Spanish also had a mission near here called Santissimo Nombre de Maria. It was four miles east of Weches on Highway 21, and it was destroyed by a flood in 1692. There is a marker at the site.

The Mission Tejas State Park is one of the state's Class I parks, with provisions for camping and picnicking, fishing and hiking. The usual charge of $1.00 per vehicle applies unless you have an annual permit or the parklands' passport.

There were no major battles between settlers and Indians in

1 *1) Mary Allen College began in Crockett when this building was opened in the late 1880s. It originally was a college for black women, sponsored by the Presbyterians. The school changed scope and character over the years. It was a Baptist college for a while before it closed in the late 1970s.*

this area. But several white settlers were killed by Indians in the early 1830's in the northern end of what is now Houston County. It happened near a settlement known as Augusta, and it came to be known as the Eden-Madden massacre. Augusta has vanished. The site of the massacre is now private property and not readily accessible. There are markers in a little park on Farm Road 227, about 10 miles east of Grapeland.

Most of the eastern end of Houston County is in the Davy Crockett National Forest. There are two designated recreation areas in the forest within this county. Neches Bluff on the west bank of the Neches River off Highway 21 on Forest Service Road 511 has provisions only for picnicking and hiking. But the Ratcliff Lake Recreation Area, off Highway 7 between Kennard and Ratcliff, has provisions for camping, swimming and boating, and there are some shelters for rent. There is an admission fee at the Ratcliff Lake Recreation Area.

2) This is a familiar scene to anyone who travels much through Angelina County. More than half of the county is in commercial forests and the south-eastern corner of the county is covered by the Angelina National Forest. 2

ANGELINA COUNTY

The earliest Spanish missionaries in East Texas met and converted to Christianity a young Hanina Indian girl. She helped the missionaries convert other Indians. She learned the Spanish language and generally made herself so agreeable to the newcomers that they began calling her The Little Angel, or Angelina. In some other stories, the Indian lady comes off a bit more assertive and even bossy, so she may not have deserved the title completely. But she was known as Angelina. The village where she lived became Angelina's Village, and the river bedside it became the Angelina River.

Angelina County was named for the river when it was established in 1846. Timber is the big resource and the big business here. Substantially more than half the land in the county is in commercial forests. The Sam Rayburn Reservoir forms the eastern boundary of the county, and the Angelina

1

1) *The Texas Forestry Association maintains this museum next to its headquarters in Lufkin. It brings together relics and artifacts that tell of the early days of Texas' big lumber industry. This industry provided the lumber to build the homes and businesses that spread across East and Central Texas in the years that followed the Civil War.* 2) *Angelina County's modern courthouse at Lufkin was built in 1955. Lufkin got its start from an imaginative real estate promotion.*

2

National Forest covers the southeastern corner of the county.

Lufkin is the county seat. The present courthouse was built in 1955. Lufkin became a town almost by accident, and it was not named for an angel.

Angelina County had three other county seats before Lufkin. A town named Marion was the original county seat. The county government moved from there to Jonesville in 1854 and then moved in 1858 to a town named Homer. The story they tell about what happened to Homer is that some railroad workmen got boisterous there one night while they were building a railroad through the county in the early 1880's. The railroad men were arrested and their boss decided he would not lay any tracks through a town where the authorities were so lacking in understanding. The tracks were laid six miles to the northwest of Homer and the town that grew up beside the tracks was named for railroad man E. P. Lufkin. He was the boss of the crew arrested by the authorities in Homer. The railroad was the Houston, East and West Texas line. That line and the Kansas City and Gulf Short Line put on a big real estate promotion and ran excursions and served barbecue and persuaded a number of people that Lufkin was

3) Boykin Creek Recreation Area is at Boykin Springs, 14 miles southeast of Zavalla on Forest Service Road 313. 3

going to be a city. The buyers of the lots moved in and made it a city. It became the county seat in 1892.

The original stands of timber around here began to play out around the turn of the century. It has been estimated that more than one billion feet of long leaf pine was cut and hauled out of the forests in this one county in the single year of 1890. Many of the early lumber towns folded up and died as the timber played out. But Lufkin had a railroad and some manufacturing plants. It has since become a major manufacturing center and the timber has come back, too. The timber companies began replanting the forests in the 1930's. The four big timber operators now try to grow as much timber each year as they cut during the year. The four big operators in East Texas are Champion, Southland, Kirby and Temple. In the late 1890's, the Temple Company established a sawmill in Diboll reputed to be the biggest in Texas at the time. The company is still in Diboll operating a big plywood plant. Temple is now called Temple-Eastex, and it is a division of Time, Incorporated. Arthur Temple is the biggest single stockholder of Time as a result of the stock exchange that made the timber company a part of the magazine empire.

The Texas Forestry Association has its headquarters in Lufkin, at Atkinson and Oleta Streets, off State Highway 103. The association maintains a forestry museum next door to its headquarters. There is a collection of photographs and relics and artifacts inside and some heavy equipment from the early days of the lumber industry outside. The museum is open weekday afternoons, and there is no charge.

1

1) White-tailed deer populate the forests of East Texas. They are often observed in heavily-forested areas like this one in Angelina County. You are more likely to see them between hunting seasons. The hunting season usually is in November and December.

Somebody gave Lufkin businessman Walter Trout a hippopotamus as a Christmas present a number of years ago. The gift gave Trout the idea that Lufkin should have a zoo. He convinced the City Council and the result was the Ellen Trout Zoo, at Loop 287 North and Lake Street.

A major event in Lufkin every year is a carnival they call the Hush Puppy Olympics. It is usually the last Saturday in May.

The big industries in Lufkin are Lufkin Industries and Southland Paper Mills. But Texas Metal Casting Company has been attracting some attention with a cake pan made in the shape of the state of Texas. The pans are made here, but they are not for sale at the factory. Several stores around the state sell them.

Lake Sam Rayburn is the largest artificial lake in the state of Texas, not counting lakes on the borders. Lake Sam Rayburn has more than 500 miles of shoreline. Almost half of this is in Angelina County. Zavalla on U.S. 69 south of Lufkin is the gateway to the Angelina National Forest Recreation Areas on the lake in this county.

Zavalla is a lumber town more than 100 years old. There is a typical early East Texas log house here near the intersection of U.S. 69 and Farm Road 1270. It was built by a settler named Henry Havard more than 100 years ago. Havard's great grandson, Joe Tatum, lives nearby. If you can find him he might show you inside the old cabin.

The recreational areas in the National Forest around Zavalla are:

- Boykin Springs, 14 miles southeast of Zavalla by way of State Highway 63 and Forest Service Road 313. There are shelters and provision for camping, swimming and picnicking, and there is a fee.
- Letney, 25 miles southeast of Zavalla by way of State Highway 63, Farm Road 255 and Forest Service Road 335

2

3

2) Henry Havard built this log house more than a century ago. It stands near where US 69 and Farm Road 1270 meet at Zavalla. 3) Shirley Creek Park in Angelina County attracts the serious fresh-water fisherman.

with shelters and provisions for camping, swimming and picnicking. There is a fee.

● Caney Creek Recreation Area, 14 miles southeast of Zavalla by way of State Highway 63 and Farm Road 2743 with shelters and provisions for camping, swimming and picnicking. There is a fee.

● Sandy Creek, 14 miles southeast of Zavalla by way of State Highway 63 and Forest Service Road 333 with shelters and provisions for camping, swimming and picnicking. There is a fee.

● Bouton Lake, 15 miles southeast of Zavalla by way of State Highway 63 and Forest Service Road 303 with provisions for picnicking, camping and boating. There are no shelters and there is no fee here.

The Highway Department distributes a guide to public campgrounds in Texas. It lists all of the campgrounds maintained by state, federal or local government agencies. Copies

1

1) The San Augustine County Courthouse in San Augustine is only a few blocks from where the Spanish built their first mission in this area in 1717. There has been discussion about building a replica of that mission on the original site.

can be obtained free by writing to the Travel and Information Division of the State Department of Highways and Public Transportation, Post Office Box 5064, Austin 78763.

SAN AUGUSTINE COUNTY

This is one of the original counties established by the First Congress of the Republic of Texas right after the end of the Revolution in 1836. The county was named for the municipality the Mexicans had established here earlier. The city of San Augustine is the county seat. The present courthouse was built in 1927.

The first Europeans to set foot in this area may have been members of the Moscoso Expedition. Luis de Moscoso de Alvarado took over command of Hernando de Soto's expedition when De Soto died on the banks of the Mississippi in 1542. Moscoso and his men are believed to have wandered around his part of Texas for a while trying to find their way to Mexico. They eventually gave up the idea of walking there. They built some boats and sailed to Mexico.

The area here was inhabited by the Ais Indians when the Spanish priest Antonio Margil de Jesus established the Mission Nuestra Senora de los Dolores de los Ais in 1717 where the city of San Augustine is now. Nobody liked the Ais Indians very much. The Caddo Indians distrusted them and so did the Spanish and the French. The site of the mission the Spanish built for them is four blocks south of the courthouse square in San Augustine. Nothing is left of the mission, but there are plans for a replica on the original site.

A specialist in authentic restoration work lives in San Augustine. Architect Raiford Stripling has his office in the old San Augustine jail. He supervised the restoration of Ashton Villa in Galveston and the Presidio La Bahia in

2) The Ezekiel Cullen House in San Augustine was built in 1839 and it is considered one of the best early examples of Greek Revival architecture in the state. Cullen's grandson made a fortune in the oil business and gave the house to the Daughters of the Republic of Texas for preservation. 3) This old bell was dug up at the site where the Mission Dolores de los Ais was located.

Goliad. Stripling is working on plans for restoring the Mission Dolores.

One of Stripling's earlier restorations is on Highway 21, 10 miles west of the city of San Augustine. He restored to its original condition the log house Milton Garrett built beside the Old San Antonio Road in 1826. It is on the south side of the road. It is not open to the public.

Many more old buildings probably would be standing in San Augustine today except for a big fire that destroyed much of the town in 1890.

Several very old buildings do still stand here. The Ezekiel W. Cullen home at Congress and Market was built in 1839. It is a large frame building of the Greek Revival style. It has six rooms and a ballroom occupying the entire second floor. Ezekiel Cullen was a Judge of the First District Court. He was the grandfather of Hugh Roy Cullen. Hugh Roy made a for-

1

2

1) Matthew Cartwright's House in San Augustine is another example of quality frontier architecture. It was built in the 1830s. 2) Christ Episcopal Church was established here in 1848. This building has been here since 1870.

tune in oil, and he presented his grandfather's home to the Daughters of the Republic of Texas in 1953. The home is open to the public daily during the summer months and on weekends and by appointment the rest of the year. There is no admission charge, but donations are welcome.

Some of the other old homes here are open during the annual Antique Show and Tour of Medallion Homes and Historic Places in June.

There are more than four dozen historical medallions and markers on buildings in and around San Augustine.

The home Matthew Cartwright built in 1839 at 912 Main Street and the Ezekiel Cullen house both are listed in the National Register of Historic Places.

The Christ Episcopal Church here is said to be the oldest Episcopal Church in Texas. It was established in 1848. The present building on South Ayish Street between Main and Market was built in 1870. The pews are the originals, made by hand. One of the organizers of this church was Mrs. J. Pinckney Henderson. She was the wife of the first Governor of the state of Texas.

The Memorial Presbyterian Church here is said to be the oldest Presbyterian Church in Texas. It was organized in 1838. The present building at 620 Livingston was built in 1887.

A retired pharmacist named L. W. Jones is a very popular figure with the young people around San Augustine. Jones imitates locomotive and steam whistles. He can draw a crowd of youngsters anytime he appears on the courthouse lawn. They call him Casey Jones.

3

3) Memorial Presbyterian Church in San Augustine is thought to be the oldest church of this denomination in Texas. This building was built in 1887. 4) Architect Raiford Stripling of San Augustine put this old cabin back in its original condition. Milton Garrett built it originally in 1826.

4

There are two recreation areas in the Angelina National Forest convenient to San Augustine. The Townsend Recreation Area is on Lake Sam Rayburn, five miles northwest of Broaddus by way of State Highway 147 and Farm Roads 1277 and 2923.

The Harvey Creek Recreation Area is on the lake, nine miles east and south of Broaddus by way of Farm Road 83 and Farm Road 2390.

SABINE COUNTY

Sabine County is one of the original counties created by the First Congress of the Republic in 1836. The name comes from the Sabine River. Sabine is the Spanish word for cypress.

1

2

1) It is not unusual to find local citizens enjoying shade trees around the courthouse square in any small Texas town. At Hemphill, in Sabine County, they still play checkers on the courthouse grounds. 2) The Sabine County Courthouse was built in 1908. The aluminum windows and asphalt shingle roof were put on later.

About half of Sabine County lies within the Sabine National Forest. The forest was established by the U.S. Forest Service as part of the program to revive the forests after the lumber companies had cut down most of the original timber. The Sam Rayburn Lake touches the southwest corner of the county. The Toledo Bend Reservoir lies along the entire eastern edge of the county. Louisiana is on the other side of the reservoir.

The principal occupations here are farming, ranching, lumbering and catering to the fishermen. The Chamber of Commerce office on Highway 184 just off the square in Hemphill has information about the many fishing resorts in the county.

Hemphill has been the county seat of Sabine County since 1858. The present courthouse was built in 1908, but it has been changed and remodeled. The county jail building sits on one corner of the courthouse grounds. The jail was built in 1905 and it does not appear to have had anything done to it since then. There is a gallows in the little tower, but it has

3) A deputy holds an old ball and chain that will go into Hemphill's antique jail. 4) It will become a museum when a new jail is built.

been boarded up. The county is planning to build a new jail and this old building may become a museum then.

The original county seat was Milam. It is the oldest town in the county. There is not much to Milam today, but it was an important town in the early days. Highway 21 crosses the Toledo Bend Reservoir on a very long bridge here. Highway 21 was the original San Antonio Road. Where the reservoir is now, the Sabine River was. Where the bridge is, the Gaines Ferry was. The ferry was established by James Gaines about 1819. Many of the early settlers of Texas came through Milam. Stephen F. Austin came in this way. Milam was one of the principal ports of entry during the years before and during the Civil War. There were two race tracks here once and a number of inns and taverns. The town went into a decline when the county seat was moved to Hemphill.

The Mexicans tried to prevent Anglos from settling this close to the border during the colonial period. The early official colonies were all farther west. Settlers in the official colonies were all required to profess Catholicism. The unauthorized settlers in the areas here close to the Louisiana border did as they pleased about religion and some of them held Protestant services. Methodist services were held in the early 1830's in the home of Samuel McMahan a few miles west of Milam. The group meeting at McMahan's organized as a religioius society in 1833. They organized a Methodist Church the following year and built their first building in 1839. The present McMahan's Chapel Church was built in 1949. This is said to be the oldest Methodist Church in continuous existence in Texas and it may be the oldest Protestant church in

1

2 *1) Sport fishing is almost an industry in Sabine County where Toledo Bend Reservoir draws anglers from all over. 2) This marker recalls an early Spanish army post and 3) this one is on the oldest continuously-occupied site in East Texas.* 3

Texas. There is a granite marker on Highway 21, 10 miles west of Milam. But the church is two miles south on Spur 35.

The Red Hills Recreation Area in the Sabine National Forest is just north of Milam off State Highway 87. There are shelters and provisions for camping, swimming and fishing. There is an admission fee.

There are three recreation areas in the Sabine National Forest southeast of Hemphill. The Indian Mounds Recreation Area is on Toledo Bend Reservoir, about 12 miles southeast

4) Sabine National Forest sprawls over a sizable part of Sabine County and areas like the Willow Oak Recreational Area are popular with campers and nature lovers. 4

of Hemphill by way of Farm Road 83 and Forest Service Roads 115 and 115A. There are shelters and provisions for camping, swimming, boating and fishing. There is an admission fee.

The Lakeview Primitive Camping Area is on the reservoir, 16 miles southeast of Hemphill by way of State Highway 87 and a local road that is not very well marked. There is no fee here.

The Willow Oak Recreation Area is on the reservoir about 14 miles southeast of Hemphill by way of State Highway 87 and Forest Service Road 117. There are provisions for camping, swimming and fishing, but no shelters.

Pineland in the southwestern corner of the county is the biggest town in Sabine County. It has been an important sawmill center for nearly 100 years, and it still is.

TYLER COUNTY

Tyler County was organized in 1846 and named for President John Tyler. The county seat is Woodville, and it was named for George Tyler Wood because he introduced the bill creating the county while he was serving in the Senate. The present courthouse at Woodville was built in 1894, and remodeled in 1936.

The site where Woodville is today was chosen to be the county seat when the county was formed. There was no town here, and what happened next was similar to what happened in several other Texas counties. Dr. Josiah Wheat gave the county 200 acres of land. The new county government held a

1

2

These photos show the Tyler County Courthouse at Woodville 1) as it looks today and 2) as it looked in the 1890s. Remodeling came in 1936.

3

3) Former Governor Allan Shivers and his wife bought this Victorian home and donated it to the city of Woodville to be used as a museum and library. It is at 302 North Charlton Street.

public auction and sold off lots. The money from the sales went into the county treasury to pay for the courthouse and other public buildings, and the city and county were launched. The Texas and New Orleans Railroad put a line through here in the 1880's and hauled out great quantities of timber. Lumbering still is one of the principal activities here. There is some oil and gas production, too, and some agriculture.

Former Governor Allan Shivers was born near Woodville and grew up here. He and Mrs. Shivers bought and restored and gave to the people of Woodville a number of years ago an old Victorian home. It is open to the public now as the Allan

4

5

6

4) In Tyler County there lives and works one of the few professional whittlers still going strong. Sid Owens practices his craft at the eastern edge of Woodville, on US 190. 5) John Henry Kirby of Tyler County was one of the big names in East Texas timber. 6) The Heritage Garden is just west of Woodville on US 190.

Shivers Library and Museum. It is at 302 North Charlton Street. The museum is open all day Mondays and Tuesdays and all afternoon Wednesdays and Fridays and also on Saturday mornings. There is an admission fee.

The B. A. Steinhagen Lake is east of Woodville on U.S. 190. The highway crosses the lake, and there are units of the Martin Dies, Jr. State Park on both sides of the lake. This is a

1

2

1) In March and April in Tyler County you can see some of the finest displays of dogwood blooms to be found anywhere in East Texas. Woodville holds a Dogwood Festival during the blooming season to celebrate the beauty of this native Texas tree. 2) John Henry Kirby built this building as a community hall for Peachtree Village in 1912. It is now the Kirby Museum. It is located near Chester.

Class I park with provisions for camping, swimming, boating and fishing. There is the usual fee of $1.00 per vehicle unless you have an annual permit or parklands' passport.

The John Henry Kirby State Forest is 14 miles south of Woodville on U.S. 69. Lumberman Kirby gave this park to the state in 1929 after he had cut most of the trees. Fortunately, the trees have grown back. There is a hiking trail and a picnic area. There is a firewatch tower visitors are allowed to climb.

There is a collection of antiques and antique buildings just west of Woodville on U.S. 190 at a place called Heritage Garden. This place is owned and operated by Clyde Gray.

3

3) This is the Enloe House nine miles east of Chester in Tyler County on FM 1745. It was built in 1852.

Clyde is an artist and ceramist and history buff. And he is a promoter. This is a commercial tourist resort. Gray charges an admission fee of $1.00 for adults. But he has some things here you may not see anywhere else. There are no replicas. The buildings are old ones moved here from their original sites. The furnishings and implements are authentically old and not restored. Gray keeps adding more exhibits. He has acquired the old clock that was made for the city hall in Houston in the 1890's. He has put it back in working condition and installed it in a special tower at Heritage Village. He has moved an old schoolhouse to the village and turned it into a boarding house. Country food is served here, family style. The cornbread is made from meal ground in the village the old way. There is no better cornbread.

Probably the earliest European settlement in this area was a fort the Mexican government established near the mouth of Shawnee Creek in the northern end of Tyler County. This was Fort Teran. The purpose of it was to discourage further immigration from the United States. The Mexican government adopted that as a policy in 1830 and Fort Teran was built in 1831. The garrison was Mexican, but the commander was an American named Peter Ellis Bean. He had sided with Mexican revolutionaries during Mexico's struggle for independence from Spain and the Mexicans made him a colonel. Bean may have given a little unofficial help and encouragement to the Texas revolutionaries after he took over the Mexican garrison at Nacogdoches following the Battle of Nacogdoches. Fort Teran fell into ruins after that. There is only a little park and state marker at the site now. It is off Farm Road 1745, 11

1

1) Virgin timber is almost gone from the great East Texas pine tracts and longleaf pines are increasingly rare. This is why Champion International set up this hiking trail through one of the surviving stands of longleaf pine.

miles northeast of Chester. A pleasant spot, but not easy to find.

Lumber magnate John Henry Kirby came from Peachtree Village near Chester. He built a community hall for the village in 1912 and he brought a whole trainload of friends and admirers here for the grand opening. The community hall became a museum after Kirby died. It is not open on any regular schedule, but you can get in if you find anybody home at the caretaker's place. It is on Farm Road 2907.

Dogwood trees abound in the forests in Tyler County. The blooming season is late March and early April. Woodville holds a Dogwood Festival during the blooming season every year. The dogwood tree is native to Texas and most of the southern states. Dogwoods grow larger in Alabama and Georgia than they do in Texas. They are purely ornamental now. But the wood of the dogwood tree was in considerable demand before World War II. The wood is very smooth. It was the best material available for making shuttlecocks for textile mills until plastics came along.

POLK COUNTY

U.S. Highway 59 splits right through the middle of Polk County. This county has some oil and gas but the biggest factor in the economy still is timber.

Polk County was organized in 1846 and named for U.S. President James Polk. The county seat is Livingston. M. L. Choate donated the original 100 acres of the town site in 1846 and named the settlement for a town he was familiar with in Alabama. Livingston had a commercial district covering three blocks in 1902, but the entire district was destroyed by a fire

2

2) This is the Polk County Courthouse at Livingston. It was built in 1923. 3) Augustus Darby built this cabin in 1859 four miles west of Moscow on FM 350. His descendants still occupy it.

3

that year. There was plenty of building material handy, and the town was soon re-built. The present courthouse was built in 1923.

The vast forests here and in the other counties in the East Texas timber belt were alive with sawmills and lumber company towns in the 80's and 90's. The number of sawmills has declined drastically since then, and there are no company towns left. But there are plenty of lumber towns. Most of the towns in Polk County are lumber towns. Camden was about the last of the old-time company towns to disappear. W. T. Carter and Brother Lumber Company operated the sawmill and the town here through the 1960's. The houses and the businesses were owned by the company. And the company owned the squeaky little train that hauled the timber out to the main rail line at Moscow. The railroad was the Moscow, Camden and San Augustine. It owned one ancient passenger car, and the car was coupled to the end of the train on most of

1 *1) The old W. T. Carter & Brother Store at Camden in Polk County is now an office building for Champion International.*

its runs. It became a tourist attraction during the last few years of the Carter operation here.

Things are vastly different at Camden today. Champion International has bought up the entire town and the surrounding forest and the railroad. Camden still appears as a town on the map, but the townsite is one vast plywood plant. The boarding house and the church are gone. The antique depot is gone. The old company store has been turned into an office for the plywood plant. The old railroad passenger car has been sold to a tourist railroad in Arkansas and the Moscow, Camden and San Augustine hauls only the products of Champion International today.

A park on U.S. 59 at Moscow honors the late publisher and politician William P. Hobby. He was the grandson of Fort Bend County pioneer Dr. John Pettus and the father of Lieutenant Governor Bill Hobby. William P. Hobby was Governor from 1917 to 1921. He and his wife, Oveta Culp Hobby, bought the *Houston Post* after he left the Governor's office, and she continues to run the paper. Governor Hobby was born in Moscow.

The Polk County Memorial Museum at 601 West Church Street in Livingston has a number of exhibits dealing with the history of the county and the Alabama-Coushatta Indians.

2

3

4

2) This old courthouse annex building at Livingston was rented out for years to the law firm of Campbell and Foreman. The Foreman in that firm was Zemmie Lee, the older brother of noted Houston lawyer Percy Foreman. 3) This park near Moscow is a memorial to former Governor W. P. Hobby. 4) He was born in Moscow. The laws providing free school books and compulsory school attendance in Texas were enacted during Hobby's terms in the governor's office.

5

5) The creation of vast new bodies of fresh water in recent years has also provided major playgrounds for regions such as Polk County. These are some of the shelters now available for rent at Lake Livingston Recreation Area.

1

These are the scenes in the Big Thicket. 1) This is a portion of Big Sandy Creek as it passes through Polk County south of the Indian reservation. 2) This concentration of trees, undergrowth and boggy earth sheltered wild animals and occasional outlaws well into the 20th Century. The National Park Service in 1978 was still acquiring lands for the Big Thicket National Preserve. It will not be a park. There will be about a dozen areas scattered throughout the Thicket preserved in their natural state for hiking and day use.

2

The museum is open weekday afternoons. There is no charge, but donations are encouraged.

There is a new state park on the east shore of Lake Livingston near the city of Livingston. This is a Class I park with a number of shelters and campsites and three boat ramps. The park is southwest of Livingston by way of U.S. Highway 59, Farm Road 1988 and Farm Road 3126.

Rockhounds will want to know that The Johnson Rock Shop east of Livingston has a very big collection of petrified wood. The Johnson's place is in the Indian Springs Subdivision off U.S. Highway 190, about 10 miles east of Livingston.

The first white settlers probably arrived in this area in the early 1830's. The Alabama Coushatta Indians were already

3

3) The Big Thicket has been for many years a botanist's and nature lover's delight. The great variety of plants found in its depths have been attracting student groups and researchers to study here for many years.

here. But they were immigrants, too. The two tribes had moved from the southeastern United States as white settlers moved into their original homelands.

The white settlers of Texas dispossessed the Alabama-Coushatta, too, when they established their Republic in 1836. But the Alabamas and Coushattas always got along better with the whites than most of the other Indians did. They stayed when the Cherokees were expelled from the state in 1839. And the State of Texas bought 1,200 acres of land in Polk County in 1854 for a reservation for the Alabama-Coushattas. The reservation has been enlarged several times. The State of Texas now holds in trust for the Alabama-Coushattas 4,600 acres of land on both sides of U.S. 190, 16 miles east of Livingston.

Indian families live here in neat brick homes the tribe has built with the help of the Federal Department of Housing and Urban Development. The Indians pay rent to the tribe and the rent is based on their income. Some of them work on the reservation and some of them work for the timber companies and other industries near the reservation.

The Alabama-Coushatta Reservation is administered by the Texas Indian Commission, but the superintendent of the reservation now is a member of the tribe. Emmett Battise is second chief of his tribe and the first Indian to be superintendent here. He is a cousin of first chief Fulton Battise.

The Alabama-Coushattas were living much more modestly on their reservation here until about 1967 when they got the

1

1) The reservation of the Alabama-Coushatta Indians near Livingston is said to be the only Indian preserve in the nation administered by a state. The others are federal. Here, young members of the tribe perform dances for visitors.

idea to turn the place into a tourist attraction. They relearned some forgotten Indian crafts and developed dance programs. They established an inn to serve food to the visitors and they laid out a miniature railroad and other attractions. Their reservation is closed a few hours on Sunday mornings and for a couple of weeks at Christmas time. The rest of the time it is open and the Indians encourage visitors every way they can. They have a petting zoo and a fishing lake. There is a campground on the reservation, and they stage a program in an outdoor theater during the summer months. The program is an historical drama. It is titled "Beyond the Sundown." There is no charge for admission to the reservation or the museum. But the Indians charge admission for the historical drama, and the prices in the reservation gift shop make it plain that these Indians have learned how to cope with the paleface.

2) This is Fulton Battise, Chief of the Alabama-Coushatta Tribe. His ancestors immigrated to Texas before the white settlers did. They stayed when the Cherokees were expelled. The Indians hold open house for tourists. Visitors are welcomed at the reservation almost the year around and they present a dramatic show in their outdoor theater every evening in the summer. 2

Index

Bold type represents the location of a related photograph.